THE UNOFFICIAL ENCYCLOPEDIA OF ULTIMATE CHALLENGES FOR MINECRAFTERS

NEW ADVENTURES AND THRILLING DARES TO TAKE YOUR GAME TO THE NEXT LEVEL

MEGAN MILLER

Sky Pony Press
New York

Sky Pony Press books may be purchased in bulk at special discounts for sales promotion, corporate gifts, fundraising, or educational purposes. Special editions can also be created to specifications. For details, contact the Special Sales Department, Sky Pony Press, 307 West 36th Street, 11th Floor, New York, NY 10018 or info@ skyhorsepublishing.com.

Sky Pony® is a registered trademark of Skyhorse Publishing, Inc.®, a Delaware corporation.

Minecraft® is a registered trademark of Notch Development AB.
The Minecraft game is copyright © Mojang AB.

Visit our website at www.skyponypress.com.

Authors, books, and more at SkyPonyPressBlog.com.

10 9 8 7 6 5 4 3 2 1

Library of Congress Cataloging-in-Publication Data is available on file.

Cover design by Brian Peterson
Cover and interior art by Megan Miller

Thanks to the many Minecraft skin artists who share their work on sites like Needcoolshoes.com. The illustrations in this book use skins from users.

Print ISBN: 978-1-5107-3842-3
Ebook ISBN: 978-1-5107-3843-0

Printed in China

FOREWORD

This is a rainy-day book for Minecraft. Use it when you want to play but you've already got a base and plenty of resources and ores, and you are looking for something interesting to do—a new build, challenge, project, or gameplay style you've never tried before.

The challenges in this book include challenges from my own gameplay as well as challenges from players like you who have posted on community forums and uploaded videos of their own experiences to YouTube. Some can be played only on multiplayer. Some are short-term quests, some are contests or races, and others are ways to change your gameplay in a new world. If you aren't interested in multiplayer (though I highly recommend trying this at least once), you can achieve many of these challenges by yourself in your own private Minecraft world. A few involve playing with Minecraft mods, which I also highly recommend, as installing modpacks has become very easy.

There are also a few entries with tips on creating your own challenges: See Challenges, Role Play, Scavenger Hunt.

Each challenge entry is categorized with the following:

- Advancement—An in-game Minecraft advancement
- Building—A building challenge
- Competition—A timed or measured competition
- Gameplay—Open-ended gameplay with rules or role play added
- Maps—Involves downloading and playing a customized map
- Modded—Involves playing with a specific mod or a modpack
- OOG—Out of game; involves an activity away from the Minecraft game
- Quest—Gameplay that requires achieving a specific goal, so it has a specific end
- Server—Involves playing on a public server (may be with or without friends)
- Skill—Involves practicing some part of gameplay to become better at it
- Software—Involves using third-party software
- SMP—Multiplayer survival (requires several players to do the challenge)
- SSP—Single player survival

Also: This book of challenges is written with the Java Edition 1.12 of Minecraft in mind. However, most if not all of these challenges can be used or customized to other Minecraft editions.

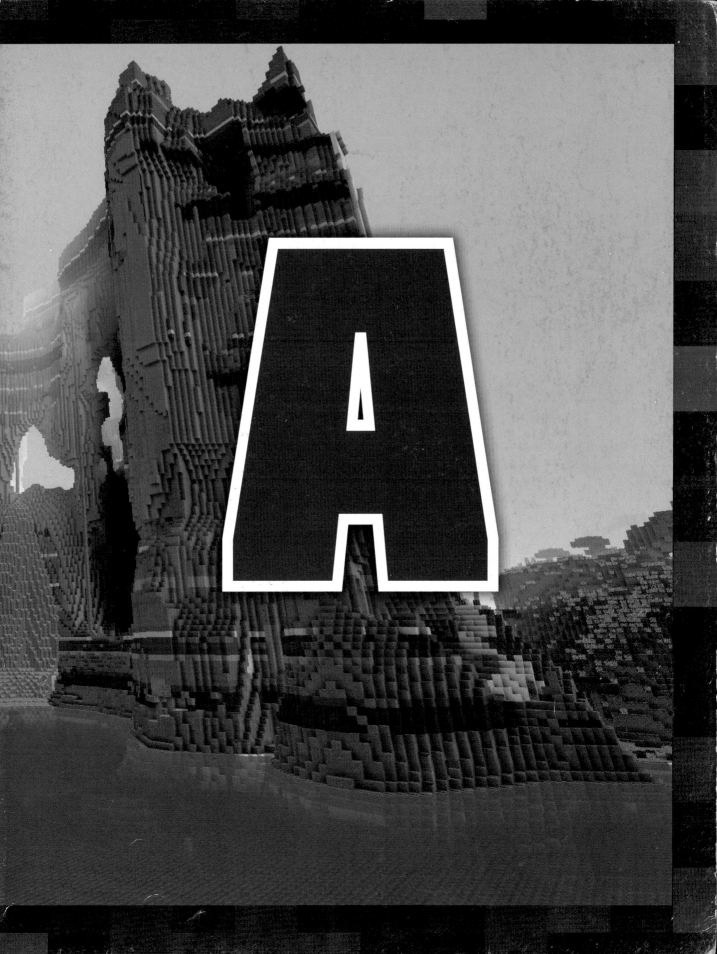

ABBA CAVING

SMP, Competition

This is a cave mining competition created by popular YouTuber VintageBeef. All players use a Silk Touch pick and start at the same cave opening at the same time. Everyone mines for an agreed-upon number of minutes, usually twenty minutes. The goal is to collect as many rare ores as possible. When the mining time is done, everyone counts points of the ores they have mined. The most points wins, and the winner takes all of the ores from all players. (Of course, it is considered good sportsmanship to gift a few diamonds to each player!) The name ABBA comes from the 1980s pop group ABBA's song, "The Winner Takes It All." Coal and iron are worthless. Additional rules include: No PvP and no strip mining except to find another cave. Potions and Ender pearls are allowed.

ABBA caving videos are also pretty fun to watch. In YouTube, search "ABBA Caving" to see VintageBeef and others compete.

- Emeralds: 7 points
- Diamonds: 5 points
- Gold: 3 points
- Lapis: 1 point
- Redstone: 1 point

Variation: Include name tags, horse armor, and golden apples found in dungeons or abandoned mineshafts, and give each a preset value between seven and fifteen points.

See also: Bedrock Drag Racing

In ABBA Caving, the Winner Takes It All!

ADVANCEMENTS, GET THEM ALL

SSP, SMP, Quest, Competition

The Minecraft advancements are a set of in-game achievements and challenges. While you will achieve most of the advancements by simply progressing through the game, it is difficult to get all the advancements.

To view the Advancements screen, press Escape and then click the Advancements button. There are currently five tabs of advancement categories: Minecraft, Nether, End, Adventure, and Husbandry. Each tab only appears on the Advancement screen when you've completed one of the tasks in its category. You don't have to complete the tasks in any order, either, although more advanced tasks may only appear in the tab after earlier ones are completed. You can complete a more advanced task before others and it will reveal earlier tasks.

There are also three difficulty levels of advancement. From easiest to most difficult, these are Normal, Goal, and Challenge advancements. The easiest tasks that will open up all the tabs are the following: make a crafting table (Minecraft tab), kill any mob (Adventure tab), and eat any food (Husbandry tab). To open the Nether and End tabs, you need to visit those dimensions.

There are a few advancements that have solutions that aren't easy or obvious. For help finishing all the Minecraft advancements, look at the individual entries for tips and explanations on these: Adventuring Time, A Balanced Diet, Monsters Hunted, The Next Generation, Two by Two, Very Very Frightening, Withering Heights, Zombie Doctor.

There are also advancements that get you a chunk of experience, too. Under Nether: Subspace Bubble (100 XP), Return to Sender (50 XP), Uneasy Alliance (100 XP), A Furious Cocktail (100 XP), How Did We Get Here (1000 XP). Under End: Great View From Up Here (50 XP). Under Husbandry: Two by Two (100 XP), A Balanced Diet (100 XP), Serious Dedication (100 XP).

A popular speedrun category is the advancements speedrun. A recent record advancement speedrun in 2017 timed at three hours,

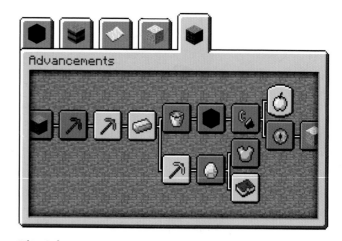

The Advancements Screen

thirty-seven minutes, and twenty-eight seconds by player Cavin856. As with other competitive speedruns, specific world seeds are used for each run. First, using a common seed sets an even playing ground for competitors and different runs (if you are playing against yourself). Second, seeds are chosen that have features that help improve the seed with which you travel to important areas, like strongholds, villages, etc.

See also: How Did We Get Here, Speedrun

ADVENTURE MAP, CREATE YOUR OWN

SSP, Quest

Minecraft maps are created by players—like you! If you have a hankering for making your own games and challenges, it is easy to get started with a basic map. To plan your map, figure out what type of map (adventure, parkour, etc.), size, and theme/challenges/story you want. The practical steps for creating a basic map are the following: (1) Create a new Minecraft world (Superflat or Void may be the easiest to customize). (2) Use a map editor to change or create the terrain and structures for your map. (3) In Minecraft creative mode, add challenges such as place mobs, traps, pitfalls, puzzles, mazes, loot, instructions, etc. (4) Add

borders to your world if necessary, with the command/worldborder set X (where X is the diameter of the world area). (5) Test your map before you upload it to a map repository site or give it to friends. For more complex maps, you will want to learn how to use redstone and command blocks to program events and make dynamic puzzles and contraptions in Minecraft.

See also: Command blocks, Redstone, World-Edit

ADVENTURING TIME

Advancement

You'll get a reward of 500 XP points for this in-game advancement! There are forty specific biomes you'll need to reach: Beach, Birch Forest, Birch Forest Hills, Cold Beach, Cold Ocean, Cold Deep Ocean, Cold Taiga, Cold Taiga Hills, Desert, Desert Hills, Extreme Hills, Extreme Hills+, Forest, Forest Hills, Frozen Deep Ocean, Frozen River, Ice Mountains, Ice Plains, Jungle, Jungle Edge, Jungle Hills, Lukewarm Ocean, Lukewarm Deep Ocean, Mega Taiga, Mega Taiga Hills, Mesa, Mesa Plateau, Mesa Plateau F, Mushroom Island, Mushroom Island Shore, Plains, River, Roofed Forest, Savanna, Savanna Plateau, Stone Beach, Swampland, Taiga, Taiga Hills, and Warm Ocean.

Minecraft doesn't tell you in the game which biomes you're missing from the list, so you may want to keep track. Most of the forty biomes you'll easily visit in your travels: Taiga, Desert, Forest, Plains, Roofed Forest, etc. The variant versions of these biomes (e.g., Birch Forest Hills, Extreme Hills+), you can also usually find near their original counterparts. The rarest of the forty biomes are the Ice, Mega Taiga, Mesa, and Mushroom Biomes. As you go looking for these, you'll most likely encounter the other biomes. If you have an Elytra and plenty of rockets to fuel your flight, your quest should go much more quickly.

```
b8d5c137-ff8d-48fd-9f5c-8300ca05052f.json - Notepad

File  Edit  Format  View  Help

{   "minecraft:recipes/building_blocks/light_blue_wool": {    "criteria": {
"has_white_wool": "2018-06-04 10:39:20 -0600"    },    "done": true  },
"minecraft:recipes/building_blocks/purple_wool": {    "criteria": {    "has_white_wool":
"2018-06-04 10:39:20 -0600"    },    "done": true  },
"minecraft:recipes/transportation/dark_oak_boat": {    "criteria": {    "entered_water":
"2018-05-25 10:17:56 -0600"    },    "done": true  },
"minecraft:recipes/building_blocks/lime_wool": {   "criteria": {    "has_white_wool":
"2018-06-04 10:39:20 -0600"    },    "done": true  },
"minecraft:recipes/building_blocks/pink_wool": {   "criteria": {    "has_white_wool":
"2018-06-04 10:39:20 -0600"    },    "done": true  },
"minecraft:recipes/building_blocks/gray_wool": {   "criteria": {    "has_white_wool":
"2018-06-04 10:39:20 -0600"    },    "done": true  },
"minecraft:recipes/building_blocks/black_wool": {    "criteria": {    "has_white_wool":
"2018-06-04 10:39:20 -0600"    },    "done": true  },
"minecraft:recipes/building_blocks/blue_wool": {    "criteria": {    "has_white_wool":
"2018-06-04 10:39:20 -0600"    },    "done": true  },
"minecraft:recipes/decorations/white_bed": {    "criteria": {    "has_white_wool": "2018-
06-04 10:39:20 -0600"    },    "done": true  },
"minecraft:recipes/building_blocks/green_wool": {    "criteria": {    "has_white_wool":
"2018-06-04 10:39:20 -0600"    },    "done": true  },
"minecraft:recipes/decorations/white_carpet": {    "criteria": {    "has_white_wool":
"2018-06-04 10:39:20 -0600"    },    "done": true  },
"minecraft:recipes/building_blocks/brown_wool": {    "criteria": {    "has_white_wool":
"2018-06-04 10:39:20 -0600"    },    "done": true  },
"minecraft:adventure/adventuring_time": {    "criteria": {    "forest": "2018-06-04
10:38:26 -0600",    "deep_ocean": "2018-05-25 10:17:32 -0600",    "beaches": "2018-05-25
10:17:33 -0600",    "desert_hills": "2018-05-25 10:16:53 -0600",    "savanna": "2018-05
-25 10:16:50 -0600",    "plains": "2018-05-25 10:16:25 -0600",    "ocean": "2018-05-25
10:17:29 -0600",    "river": "2018-05-25 10:17:18 -0600",    "desert": "2018-05-25
10:16:44 -0600"    },    "done": false  },
"minecraft:recipes/building_blocks/magenta_wool": {    "criteria": {    "has_white_wool":
"2018-06-04 10:39:20 -0600"    },    "done": true  },
"minecraft:recipes/building_blocks/orange_wool": {    "criteria": {    "has_white_wool":
"2018-06-04 10:39:20 -0600"    },    "done": true  },
"minecraft:recipes/transportation/birch_boat": {    "criteria": {    "entered_water":
"2018-05-25 10:17:56 -0600"    },    "done": true  },
"minecraft:recipes/decorations/painting": {    "criteria": {    "has_wool": "2018-06-04
10:39:20 -0600"    },    "done": true  },
"minecraft:recipes/building_blocks/light_gray_wool": {    "criteria": {
"has_white_wool": "2018-06-04 10:39:20 -0600"    },    "done": true  },
"minecraft:story/root": {    "criteria": {    "crafting_table": "2018-06-04 10:38:39 -
0600"    },    "done": true  },  "minecraft:recipes/transportation/acacia_boat": {
"criteria": {    "entered_water": "2018-05-25 10:17:56 -0600"    },    "done": true  },
```

In your Minecraft game files, under Saves and in your world folder, you'll find a folder called Advancements. In here is a .json file, which you can open with a text editor. Scroll to find the entry for adventure/adventuring time, and you will see a list of the biomes you've visited already.

AMIDST, USE THE MAPPING TOOL CALLED

OOG, *Software*

Amidst is a freeware software tool from sf-editor1 that looks at a Vanilla Minecraft seed and generates a map showing where biomes and generated structures will be found on that seed. If you don't find that cheat-y, you can use it to find villages, temples, strongholds, Mooshroom Islands, witch huts, slime chunks, and more in the world you are using. If you're looking for a seed that has villages close to spawn or some other feature in a particular location, you can generate maps using random seeds that you can then evaluate.

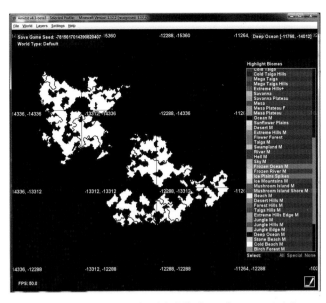

You can also choose the highlighter button and select what biomes to highlight on the map.

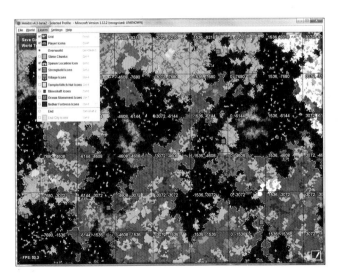

In the Amidst application, you select which seed, world, or random seed to view its map. Then you can use the Layers menu to select what structures you want to see on the map.

AMPLIFIED TERRAIN, PLAY ON

SSP, *Gameplay*

A whole new set of challenges will face you if you set your new world to "Amplified" as the world type. Amplified terrain means that the

Amplified worlds are spectacular but also make traveling around quite difficult!

land levels are exaggerated into very high cliffs and mountains. It makes for spectacular vistas, but get ready for figuring out how to traverse the lands. You'll likely be an expert at bridge building, railways, and the elytra once you've played through an Amplified world.

ANIMATION, MAKE A MINECRAFT

OOG, Software

If you've browsed YouTube for popular Minecraft videos, you've probably come across some very creative Minecraft animations and music videos. These aren't recorded inside Minecraft,

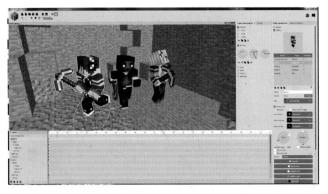

In an animation program like Mine-imator, you'll find tools to select and modify objects and characters positions for each frame (timeline), set the lighting, and more. Mine-imator includes objects for Minecraft items, blocks, and entities, so it is a good way to get started!

of course, but created frame by frame in animation programs like Blender (free), Mine-imator (free), and Cinema 4D (expensive). There

are a number of videos on YouTube showing how to animate using Blender and Mine-imator. Mine-imator is probably the easiest to start with, as it requires very little setup and is designed specifically for Minecraft settings and characters. Although it can take a bit of time to learn a 3D program and create even a fifteen-second animation, it is very rewarding creative work. There is a strong Mine-imator community and forum at mineimatorforums.com where creators share videos, objects, and more.

ARCHITECTURE, EXPLORE

SSP, Creative

Minecraft is a great creative game to explore the buildings, styles, and world of architects and architecture. You don't have to start at the beginning of history: Modern architecture, with its typically clean lines and blocky forms, can be a good way to start playing around with architectural styles. If you don't have any favorite architects or styles yet, you can search online for images of "architectural styles" or "architecture" and see what you like. Read up online or check out a library book about the architects, styles, and buildings you like. Finally, design a building in that architect's style, or recreate one of their famous buildings.

For a guide to modern architecture in Minecraft that explores several modern architects' visions and inspirations, see sarlacminecraft's guides on Imgur. Part 1 is Modern Arts and Crafts, at Imgur.com/a/q8bmq. Parts 2 (Bauhaus) and 3 (Minimalism) are linked to from the Part 1 page.

There are hundreds if not thousands of videos on YouTube explaining how to automate pretty much everything in Minecraft, including this melon farm.

This is sarlacminecraft's prairie-homed Arts and Crafts building, inspired by the works of architects like Frank Lloyd Wright and following the Arts and Crafts design concepts and values.

AUTOMATE EVERYTHING

SSP, Quest

Give up the good life of rural farming and manual resource gathering and automate everything possible. Build an automated farm or contraption for each of the following: wheat, carrots, beets, potatoes, sugar cane, cactus, cooked meat (chickens, cows, sheep, or pigs), potion brewing, doors, melons and pumpkins, flowers, XP farm, Endermen, villagers, blaze farm, squid/prismarine crystal farm, iron golem, ice, zombie pigment, slime, skeleton, spider, zombie, witch farm, creeper farm, magma cube farm.

You can find video instructions on how to build farms for each of the above on YouTube. Search for the type of farm you want to build and include the version of Minecraft you are playing. It's not uncommon for a farm working in 1.7 Java Edition to not work in 1.14 Java Edition.

Extra credit: Build a sand generator, ghast farm, and automated tree farm.

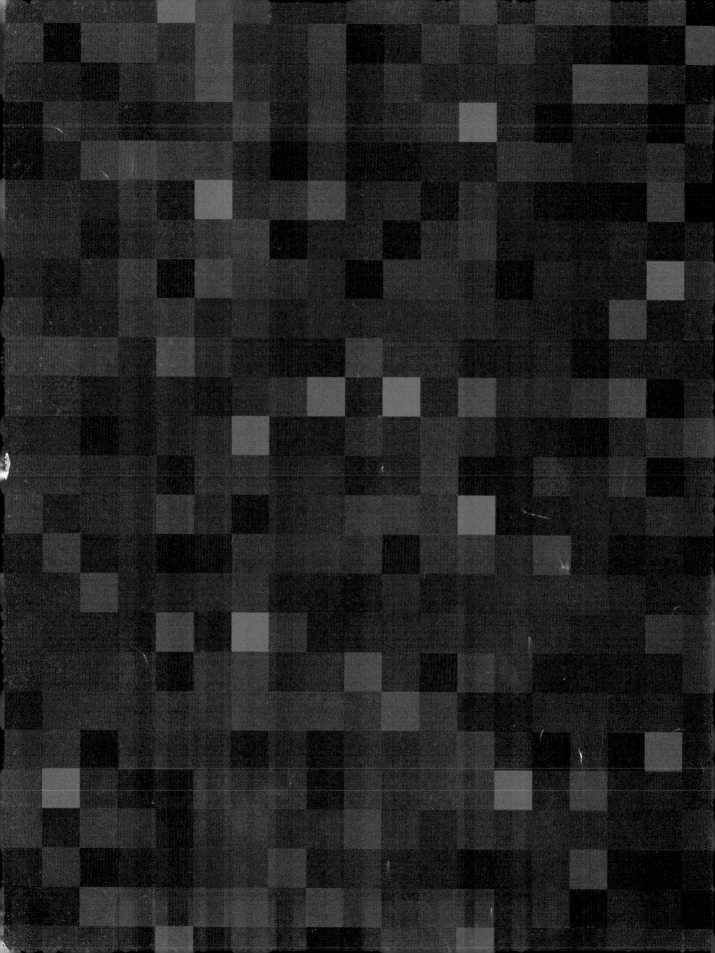

BALANCED DIET

Advancement

The in-game description for this advancement advises you to eat everything, but you can actually skip cake and milk. You do need to eat the poisonous foods, though. So, eat one of each of the following: apple (regular, golden, and enchanted golden), beetroot and beetroot soup, bread, carrot (regular and golden), chorus fruit, cookie, dried kelp, melon, mushroom stew, potato (raw, poisonous, and baked), pufferfish, pumpkin pie, rabbit stew, rotten flesh, spider eye, tropical fish, and both raw and cooked versions of beef, chicken, cod, mutton, pork, rabbit, and salmon.

BANNERS, LEARN THE ART OF MAKING CUSTOM

SSP, Creative

At first glance, the options for banner-making seem a little limited—you can add a creeper face, but not an Endermen or a zombie. However, the ability to dye up to six patterns over one another, in combination with thirty-eight patterns or symbols and sixteen colors means that you can be extremely creative with banners. It is easiest to use an online tool to mix and match layers and preview the effects—one such tool is Needcoolshoes.com/banner. You can find great examples of banners at Planet minecraft.com/banners.

Here's a banner of a fox by mr.crafteur and one of a bubbling cauldron by lovelylynea.

BEDROCK DRAG RACING

SMP, Competition

This mining competition was invented by You-Tuber generikb and is a variation on ABBA caving. It was designed for a world that has a world border, but it can be adapted as you like. In this game, participants dig in a straight line at y Level 6 from one edge of the world to the other. Caves found along the way can be explored, but no strip mining is allowed. You can climb over lava pools, but you have to dig back down to Level 6 once you've passed them.

Other rules: There is no time limit—the game ends when all players reach the end, but the first to reach the finish line gets a bonus of 20 points. Use only stone picks or iron picks to dig stone, and determine ahead of time if enchanting (and what kind) is allowed or if you are using a Silk Touch pick for digging out ores. Also decide what armor is allowed ahead of time. (Note: don't forget torches, food, wood, and any extra resources for making more iron picks.)

In the first Bedrock Drag Racing event, points were established as follows:

- Redstone: 1 point for ore 10 redstone
- Iron: 1 point for 4 iron blocks
- Lapis: 4 points per block / or 10 ore
- Gold: 3 points per block
- Diamond: 5 points per diamond
- Emerald: 7 points per diamond

To modify Bedrock Drag Racing for a borderless world, just select a starting line (where you will dig down to y=6) and an ending line where you will stop mining.

In Bedrock drag racing, you'll only be a few blocks above bedrock—and below lava Level 11.

BINGO, PLAY MINECRAFT

SMP, Competition, Map

Minecraft Bingo is a very fun, non-PVP multiplayer mini-game created by Lorgon111. In Minecraft Bingo, you'll match PvE skills against other players to collect items and blocks from the world that match items and blocks on your Bingo card. Every player or team starts with the same Bingo card, which shows random items in a 5x5 grid. You'll need to collect five items to match a straight horizontal, vertical, or diagonal line. You can download Lorgon111's Bingo map at Minecraftworldmap.com.

Note: Make sure of the version of Minecraft you'll need to play this map. Bingo version 3.1 is ready to play with Minecraft Java Version 1.11.2.

See also: Maps

In Lorgon111's Bingo map, you'll be given a bingo card. You need to complete a full row or column (or middle diagonal) by getting all the items in the row. You can see here signs with instructions—most maps you download will have a lobby area with instructions for you to get started.

BIOME, LIVE IN ONE ONLY

SSP, Gameplay

Live in one biome only, and it can't be plains or oak or birch forests. Choose from one of the hardest biomes to live in, like one of the ice biomes or a desert. Or let the game decide, and commit to the biome you spawn in. Or roll a pair of dice to get a random biome. Or you could use the Amidst program to find a seed that has the biome you want already at spawn.

You can travel outside your biome to collect resources, but the only place you can sleep is in your biome home.

Biome Dice Roll

1. Mesa
2. Roofed forest
3. Jungle
4. Ice spikes
5. Deep Ocean
6. Frozen Ocean
7. Desert
8. Swampland
9. Mega Taiga
10. Extreme Hills
11. Ice plains
12. Savanna

See also: Amidst.

Can you make a thriving base in an inhospitable biome, like the ice plains spikes?

BIOME BOUND

SSP, Gameplay, Building

In this challenge: You can only travel one biome at a time. In each biome, you must build a base that fits the biome in some way and uses base materials from that biome. Each base must contain at least one bed, one furnace, one double chest and one crafting table, and you must sleep in your base at least one night.

If a resource you want is found only in another biome, you must step your way, one biome base at a time, to the new biome. Excluded from these are oceans; a base beside the ocean, on a beach biome, grants you access to the nearby ocean and deep ocean biomes. You can play this with friends, in a race to see who gets to the end first.

Travel one biome at a time, building a biome-appropriate home at each stop. Here's a log cabin for the Taiga Biome.

BIOMES, VISIT ALL

SSP, Quest

An Elytra will help you greatly in finding every single biome.

The Minecraft Advancement Adventuring Time has you visiting forty Overworld biomes, but there are actually more than sixty. Make a checklist of every biome in Minecraft, including End Biomes and the Nether, and visit every single one. To record your progress, you can make an in-game stone post marker for each one. Keep track of where you've found each biome, either on paper, in a chart, or using maps. You could also make a postcard for each one, from a screenshot! The additional biomes not included in the Adventuring Time list are the following:

Ice Plains Spikes, Cold Taiga M, Desert M, Savanna M, Mesa (Bryce), Mesa Plateau F M, Plateau M, Hell (The Nether), Frozen Ocean, Extreme Hills M, Extreme Hills M+, Taiga M, Mega Spruce Taiga, Sunflower Plains, Flower Forest, Birch Forest M, Roofed Forest M, Swampland M, Jungle M, Jungle Edge M, Desert M, Savanna M, Mesa Plateau M, Savanna Plateau M, Warm Deep Ocean, and End biomes of Floating Islands, Medium Islands, High Islands, and Barren Islands.

See also: Adventuring Time

BOAT RACE, BUILD AND COMPETE IN A

SMP, Competition

Challenge your friends on a multiplayer server to boat races that you build yourselves. The race can be on water, ice, or both, and can even include foot racing portions. Add obstacles to make a course more challenging: underwater tunnels, sections where you race on foot, sudden drops, tricky corners, or narrow passages. Add in a shortcut that requires special expertise to get ahead of your competitors.

BREAK NO BLOCK CHALLENGE

SSP, Gameplay

This community-generated challenge asks: How many days and how far can you go if you are unable to place any blocks except for a furnace and a crafting table? You'll have to live without placing chests or beds, building a base, or fencing animals. You can right-click to make a path and use a hoe, but you'll be honor-bound to keeping the landscape exactly as it is when you spawn in. Hint: How can you sleep without crafting a bed?

The only two blocks you can place are a furnace and a crafting table.

BROKEN LEG CHALLENGE

SSP, Gameplay

In this community challenge originally proposed by Azerk on Minecraftforum.net, you can't jump. You can't pillar up or jump out of water onto land. All you can do is hobble along using your one good leg (in a regular Minecraft walk). To keep from inadvertently forgetting or cheating, disable Jump. To do this, open your Controls settings, press the shortcut button for Jump, and press Escape to change the shortcut to none.

You can watch videos of other players misadventures with this challenge by searching for "Minecraft Broken Leg Challenge."

Variation 1: You can't sprint, either.
Variation 2: You can only sneak. No regular walking. Yikes.

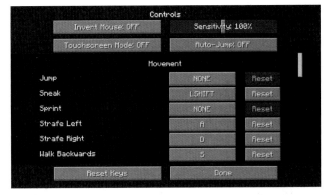

If you change the keyboard control for Jump and Sprint, you won't be able to do either.

BUILD CHALLENGES AND BATTLES, ENTER SOME

SSP, SMP, Server, Building

Minecraft communities often host build challenges; A new challenge is given every week or so, with a theme and any restrictions. Typically, anyone can enter by submitting screenshots of their creations. Planetminecraft.com has new building, skin-designing, and story challenges every month, and Reddit.com's r/Minecraft subreddit has a biweekly build challenge, for single players or build teams, with points given for first, second, and third place.

Mini-game servers like Hypixel also have timed, quick-build battles. You can compete by yourself or with a team to build something based on a random idea given to you in game. When the building time is over, players judge each other's builds and a winner is awarded!

BEDROOM, RECREATE YOUR OWN

SSP, Building

It's fun to recreate real-world locations and buildings in Minecraft, and you can start with your own home—your room, a kitchen, or some other area. You can build at scale (1 block is 1 meter, or 3.28 feet) or you can make a giant version.

In a giant version, double the scale (2 blocks is 1 meter) or go even higher. With a larger scale, you can more closely match the measurements and details in your room. Plus, it's really weird (and amusing) to walk around a giant version of your room in Minecraft. You could use your giant room as the basis of a parkour course.

To make your recreation accurate, measure your chosen room's dimensions, furniture, doors, and windows, and convert those measurements into blocks, using the scale you want. For example, a 4:1 scale (blocks to 1 meter), would mean using blocks (in each direction) instead of 1. So, a 5x5-meter bedroom at a 4:1 blocks to meters scale makes for a 20x20-block room.

BUILDING IDEAS LIST, TAKE AN IDEA FROM THIS

SSP, Building

If you have builder's block, here are some building suggestions to get your creative mind going.

- Airport
- Amusement park
- Arboretum
- Archeological dig
- Art gallery
- Battleship

- Building inspired by a book, fairy tale, movie, game, or tv show
- Cabin
- Catacombs
- City of the future
- City with canals for traveling instead of streets
- Cruise ship
- Custom forest
- Custom trees
- Dragon statue
- Dwarven underground mining kingdom
- Factory
- Farm with barns and fields
- Fishing village
- Great Wall of China
- Historic buildings from Ancient Greece, Rome, or Egypt
- Island resort
- Japanese garden
- Lighthouse
- Medieval village
- Museum
- Pagoda
- Park
- Parthenon
- Pirate cove
- Pirate ship
- Prison
- Public space for your community

- Railway system connecting points of interest or villages
- Real or imagined traditional religious building: a Buddhist temple, mosque, synagogue, church, or other
- Real-life castle
- Rollercoaster, Ferris wheel, or Minecart ride
- School
- Science laboratory
- Sculpture garden
- Sewer system
- Space colony
- Space ship
- Stadium
- Steampunk village on sky islands
- Submarine
- Swamp village
- Tree house or tree house community
- UFO
- Underwater colony
- Warehouse or industrial district
- Wizard or witch's tower
- Working water fountain
- Your ideal city

For more building inspiration, you can visit Minecraftforum.net creative forums and Planetminecraft.com's projects area to see projects that other Minecraft builders have shared.

CAPTIVE MINECRAFT, PLAY

SSP, SMP, Quest, Map

Captive Minecraft is a series of hugely popular and famous Minecraft adventure map developed by a team called the Far Landers. It's survival Minecraft with a twist. Your starting world is a single block, with world borders around you to prevent you from straying. As you accomplish various tasks, the world borders expand, giving you access to more materials for and clues to your next tasks. There are four Captive Minecraft maps out now, with more to come! Captive Minecraft IV is called Winter Realm and is designed for beginner captives.

Download the maps at Thefarlanders.com, where you can also find tips, hints, links to videos of YouTubers playing Captive Minecraft, and more.

See also: Adventure Maps

In Captive Minecraft, you'll start out with the tiniest world border ever—just one block!

CHALLENGE GENERATOR, USE A

SSP, Quest

Yes, you can use an online generator to roll virtual dice that will decide your Minecraft challenge. Go to Scenariogenerator.net/generators/minecraft. Roll for a scenario and you'll get a

Click Reroll in the Minecraft Scenario Generator to get a random biome, random restrictions, and several goals.

random biome you must build your base in, restrictions you must abide by, and tasks you must accomplish.

Example: Biome—Flower Forest. Restrictions: You can't build with planks. (Three) Goals: Collect one of every mob, kill five zombie villagers, build an item smelter.

CHALLENGES, INVENTING YOUR OWN

SSP, SMP, Quest

As you read through the challenges in this book, you'll find a few similar ideas behind many.

In a gameplay challenge (role-playing as a Looter or a Hermit or a Hobo), you impose restrictions that further the role and theme to make the game more difficult.

In scavenger challenges (Scavenger Hunt, Iron Man, Bingo, Pets, etc.), you'll decide on a set of items or blocks, which may match a theme or concept, to find.

In questing or single goal and build challenges (End Island, Fireworks, Ghast), you'll typically have just one difficult goal to achieve. Achieving the goal is an end in itself, but you can make it a race to see who achieves the goal first or gets closest to it. You may need to be very clear in defining the goal to make sure people are racing for the exact same thing.

You can use these concepts: role-playing, scavenger, and quests to make up your own challenges. If you're setting up a challenge as a competition, there are two main ways to score: whoever finishes first wins or whoever gets the most points wins.

CHUNK, BUILD YOUR BASE IN A SINGLE

SSP, Building

No more expanding bases of massive hording, no more never-ending castle fiefdoms. Embrace your inner minimalist and build your entire home within one single 16x16 chunk, and vertically as far as you need. To see where the chunks are in your world, press F3+G to toggle chunk borders on. The 3D grid shows blue, yellow, and red lines. Blue lines show each 16x16 chunk. Yellow lines show each 2x2 block area that makes up each chunk. Red lines show chunks outside of the chunk you are currently standing inside. So, find a chunk to call your own!

See also: One Chunk Challenge

The blue lines show your chunk and the yellow lines show each two-block measure within your chunk.

CHUNKY, RENDER 3D AND ISOMETRIC IMAGES WITH

SSP, Third-Party Software

Chunky is an amazing Minecraft mapping and rendering app. It is freeware created by Jesper Öqvist. It allows you to import a section of any of your Minecraft worlds and then select a portion to render. The 3D rendering engine is as good as any professional 3D program and will render a gorgeous 3D image of your Minecraft creations. Like any 3D rendering program, the higher the quality of render and the larger the area of rendering, the more CPU you'll need and the longer it'll take to render the image.

You can also use Chunky's settings to render an isometric view of your builds. In an isometric view, there's no foreshortening, so items in the distance are as large as the same items in the foreground. Isometric views work really well with Minecraft's blocky builds, showing off even the simplest builds to their best advantage. You'll often Minecraft builders' one-chunk builds rendered as isometric 3D images.

Find the app, instructions, and information at Chunky.llbit.se.

See also: One Chunk Builds

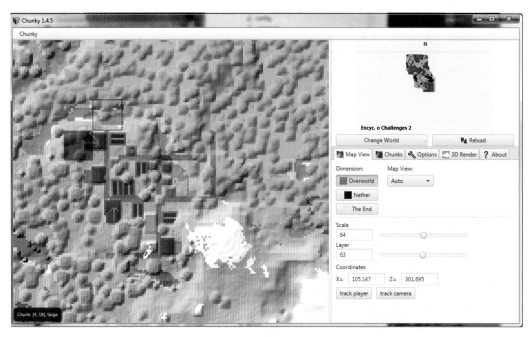

In Chunky, you first select a world, then select the chunks in that world to render.

You can see a preview of the chunks you've selected. It is easiest to use a preset camera angle.

A final render will take several minutes, up to hours, depending on the size of the area you are rendering and the level of lighting and other rendering qualities.

CITY, BUILD YOUR OWN

SSP, Building

Building your own city (or town or village) from scratch is a classic Minecraft build self-challenge. As with any large, creative builds, building a city can be tremendously satisfying if you enjoy building stuff. Although it's substantially easier to do with friends, you can definitely do this on your own, although you may want to scale this to a village with shorter buildings. If you are working in creative mode, with building mods, or with a world editor like WorldEdit, you'll be able to do more in a smaller time. If you do build your city in survival mode, you will be able to humbly brag, "Yeah, I built this all in survival!"

Also, as with large builds, planning helps make a build go much smoother. With a city, you'll want to figure out if you want to work with slopes and hills, or if it makes more sense to flatten out an area. Will you want a gridded layout, with rectangular and/or square blocks? Or do you want windy lanes and narrow alleyways? Will your city have modern buildings with different styles or buildings that look similar, as if they were built in the same era with the same materials? Define the characteristics of your city ahead of time, during the planning stage. The planning stage can be just as much fun as the building!

Area/size (City, village, or town)

Sections/Zoning: Do you want commercial, farming, industrial, and housing areas separate? Or should shops and houses intermingle?

Number of buildings

Heights of buildings

Size of buildings

Palette: Should any blocks be allowed or should the buildings be created with a limited set of blocks, or palette?

Road sizes and placement: Grids or haphazard? A main street with offshoots?

Style: There are so many to choose from. You can leave each building to its builder's choice, or go for a real-life, historical, or fictional theme: modern, medieval, eastern, SkyBlock, steampunk, underwater, space colony, fishing village, fortified/castle, fantasy, futuristic, Inuit igloo, dwarven mining village, and more.

There's a wealth of ideas and tactics on building a city in Minecraft online; Search "Minecraft building a city."

See also: WorldEdit

CITY CONSTRUCTION CHALLENGE

SSP, Quest

If you'd like a longer series of building quests in Minecraft, without being limited in the resources you can gather, try the popular City Construction Challenge on Minecraftforum.net by Iamchris27. Although there's a fairly long list of quests and requirements, the building tasks are well thought out. The overall goal is to progress at your own speed through the stages of building a city, beginning with simple huts and ending with a kingdom.

COBBLE GENERATION, LEARN THE ART OF

SSP, Skill

In SkyBlock and modded Minecraft, as well as some challenges and adventure maps, cobble generators can be the equivalent to fire in real world survival. Your ability to bend the forces of lava and water to create cobble from nothing (and avoiding creating obsidian) can mean the difference between a somewhat slow early-game progression and a VERY VERY slow game progression. You'll find a host of cobble generator examples on the Internet and YouTube. Pick one or two and learn to build them quickly from scratch, and you'll have a real advantage in certain scenarios. Here are a few simple ones.

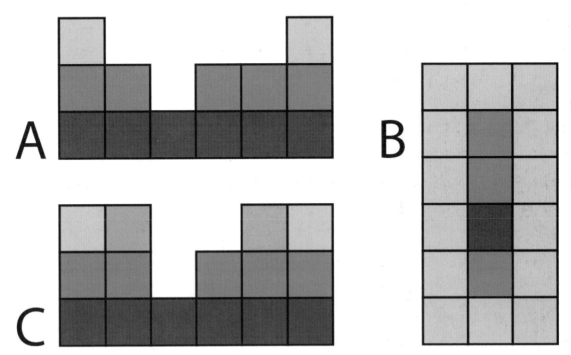

In the most basic cobble generator, you have water flowing one block out and down from the source, and a lava source two blocks away. The block in between these two flows is where the cobble is formed.

A finished basic cobble generator.

In this double-cobble cobble generator, a single source of water flows down two separated channels.

A single source of lava is placed a block away from both water flows.

Two blocks of cobble to be mined are generated from the two water flows.

COMMAND BLOCKS, LEARN

SSP, Skill

A whole new world of modifying Vanilla Minecraft and creating games, quests, and effects opens up when you learn how to program command blocks. Command blocks are redstone blocks that are available only in creative mode. To get one command block in creative mode, type the following in chat:

/give @p command_block

Right-clicking on a command block opens up an interface in which you can add a text command. When the command block is activated with a redstone signal, the command is performed.

Command blocks can perform hundreds of creative mode commands, including giving players items automatically, adding text to a player's chat, teleporting players to new locations, changing the weather and time of day, spawning mobs and custom mobs, and much more. They can be chained in sequences to perform complex if-then actions, and they are an essential part of highly custom and unique Adventure maps.

It's not hard to get started with command blocks, and you can find command generators

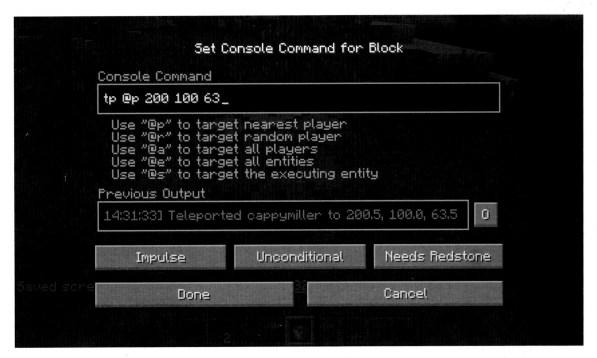

Right-click a command block to enter a command in the text box. Here is a command to teleport the nearest player to a set of coordinates.

online for creating unique mobs and more. To learn how to program command blocks, there are numerous online blog posts, YouTube videos, and books to help you get started. You'll also want to learn some redstone, too, to aid in connecting and initiating block sequences.

A simple command block project to start off with is a teleporter. Use command blocks to teleport players to important areas in your world: spawn, a Nether portal, a stronghold, and player bases.

See also: Redstone

This pressure plate will activate the command block, teleporting the player standing on it to the new location.

CREATIVE MAPS, EXPLORE CUSTOM

SSP, Maps

Teams of professional or near-professional Minecraft builders work together to create the unbelievably gorgeous and stunning maps

you'll find highlighted on Mojang's website, in YouTube fly-throughs, and pinned on Pinterest. Players like you also build creative maps and share them online at community sites like Planetminecraft.com and Minecraftforum.net

Don't confine yourself to just looking at screenshots or videos of the creations. They're made so that you can download the worlds, open them in Minecraft, and explore or live in them.

Some creation maps are also made so that you can use a world editor like WorldEdit to cut and paste buildings, trees, and other structures into your own world. Make sure that this is the purpose of the creators when you do this.

When you download a map, check the version of Minecraft it is made for and make sure to open it using the right version.

Here are a few of the amazing maps you can download from Planetminecraft.com:

- Game Board of the Ancients by Phain
- 1:2 scale of Chicago by Koodoo25
- The recreation of the Earth: 1:1500 scale (version 2.1)
- Celtanis: a massive, working Minecraft city

You can also find many creation maps at Minecraftmaps.com.

See also: World-Edit

This is a 3D rendering of Celtanis, a massive city you can download from Planetminecraft.com

CUSTOM TERRAIN, GENERATE

SSP, Gameplay

Build your next world using Minecraft's custom terrain settings to create your perfect world! In Minecraft 1.12.2, there are settings for what structures (mineshafts, ravines, ocean monuments, etc.) you want spawned, the biome sizes, river sizes, sea levels and number of lakes, ore distribution, and the way land generation stretches, flattens, or compresses land height and terrain.

For descriptions of all of these settings, visit Minecraft.gamepedia.com/customized. To use these settings, choose the Customized world type and click Customize. This will open four pages of settings you can alter to define your world generation.

You can also search for presets that other users have generated and shared, with "Minecraft world presets." In later versions of Minecraft, starting with 1.13, the way presets and custom generation may change, but you should still be able to customize your world, and you may find updated custom terrain generators as well.

On the first page of the Customize World Settings, you can select what structures are generated, biome sizes, river sizes, and more.

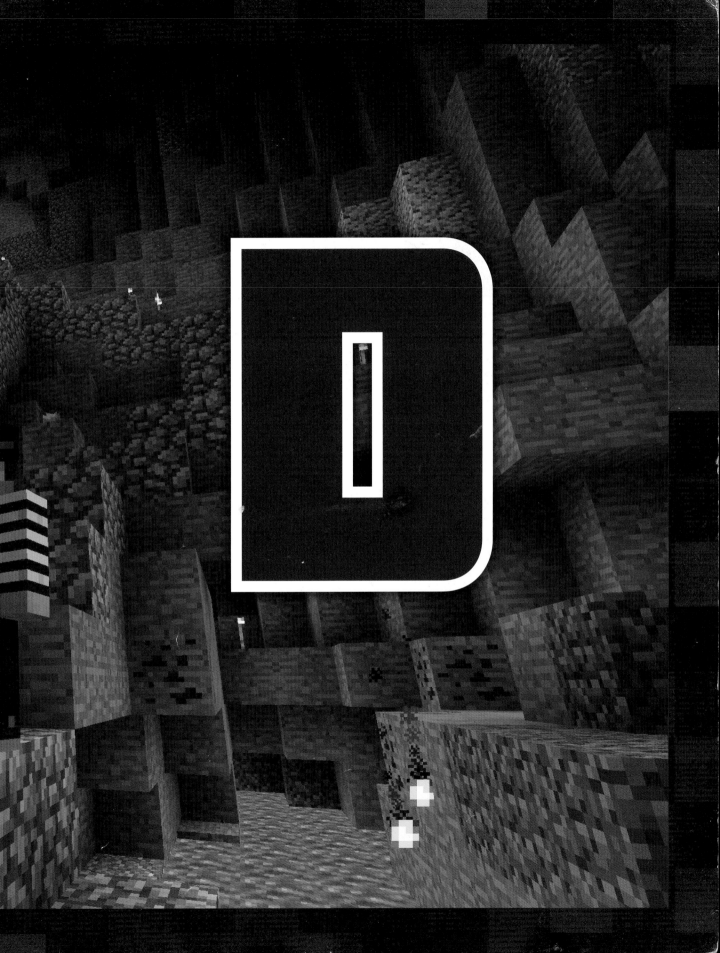

THE DROPPER, PLAY

SSP, Server, Map, Mini-game

The Dropper is one of the most famous Minecraft maps to play. Created in 2011 by Bigre, the Dropper has spawned an entire genre of mini-games and additional dropper maps. The premise is that you fall down a series of dizzying, mind-bending, vertical, tunnel-like structures. Your goal is, while falling at breakneck speed, to notice and avoid obstacles in your way and land safely. The original Dropper map can be downloaded from Minecraftforum.net, but you can find Bigre's updated map at 9minecraft.net. You can also find other dropper maps at map collection sites, and the mini-game server Hivemc.com has its own version of Dropper called Gravity.

DWARVEN HEARTSTONE

SSP, Gameplay

The Dwarven Heartstone challenge was created by Icalasari as a variant of the tree spirit challenge. You first choose one type of stone (not stone or an ore) as your heartstone. Cobblestone is a good choice! You are allowed to gather materials from a single tree and then you must start your mine. Inside your mine, place one stone block as your heartstone. From there, build your heartstone out with the same material. From now on, you can only ever be one block away from your heartstone. What is a heartstone? Different myths, old and new, treat the hearthstone of dwarves in different ways. In many, it is a magical stone that gives life to a dwarf. See Icalasari's original challenge, "Dwarven Heartstone Challenge," along with a fleshed-out backstory and rules and restrictions at Minecraftforum.net.

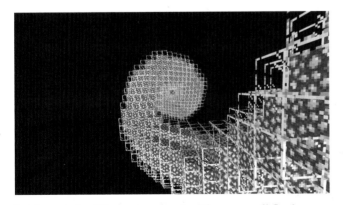

In the original Dropper map by Bigre, you'll find yourself falling through a dizzying assortment of maps—you'll want to aim for those water blocks!

In this challenge, you have to stay on a block of your chosen stone that is linked all the way back to your original heartstone.

ECONOMY SERVER, PLAY ON AN

SMP, Gameplay, Server

Economy is a whole new way to play multiplayer survival. On an economy server, you'll be rewarded with some type of currency as you perform tasks or sell goods. Generally, the lucre you earn enables you to buy more stuff that, in turn, helps you earn even more lucre and ways to make it even faster. You can find lists of economy servers at Minecraftservers.org, Minecraft-server-list.com, Minecraft-mp.com. There will be different rules and goals at different servers. At Minesaga.org, you'll be given your own sky island and a 100x100 area

to build up, make farms, sell crops and loot, climb ranks, PvP for loot, mine for money, get perks, and more. There are daily rewards if you vote for the server on popular server lists and other perks. On the other hand, you'll also get a fairly constant stream of entreaties to use your own real-life money to buy extra perks. But it is pretty easy to ignore the in-chat advertisements and concentrate on your own game. Overall, a SkyBlock economy server is a great way to get started with simple, automated redstone farms for mob grinding and loot collecting. Longtime Minecraft YouTubers VintageBeef and docm77 both have entertaining Let's Play series about making auto farms on MineSaga.

Many economy servers have a spawner economy. You work to acquire spawners, build spawner farms, and then sell the loot from your farms. In this simple iron golem farm, iron golems from multiple spawners are pushed to an opening where they drop into a fire trap. The fire trap kills them without killing their drops, and bushels of iron accumulate.

ELYTRA COURSE, BUILD AND RACE ON AN

SSP, SMP, Competition

Test your skills and your friends' with custom-built Elytra flying obstacle courses. Plan your starting jump-off spot and your final landing pad and then the general route you want to take. Obstacles can include:

- Hoops of different sizes and at different heights to fly through
- A passageway belowground that drops down and then back up again
- Short in-air tubes to pass through: horizontal, vertical, or diagonal
- Slalom-style posts that need to be passed on one side only

- Difficult or tight turns between hoops
- Obstacles of blocks and builds that prevent a flyer from taking an easier turn

If needed, include large arrows made of blocks to show flyers the direction to the next hoop.

Lots of YouTubers have created their own Elytra courses and there are also many downloadable Elytra challenge maps to download and play. Search Google or YouTube for "Elytra course Minecraft" and "Minecraft flying course."

END ISLANDS, VISIT THEM WITHOUT DEFEATING THE DRAGON

SSP, Quest

If you are determined to not engage in the End battle with the Ender Dragon, you can still reap the benefits of the End Islands and even acquire a precious Elytra. You'll need to either build a very long, many-blocked bridge away from the central island or use a flying contraption. Small flying contraptions are not hard to build, and there are many videos on YouTube with instructions for different versions of Minecraft. They typically require a few pistons and some slime blocks. Learn how to build one and practice before you set off. Once in the End,

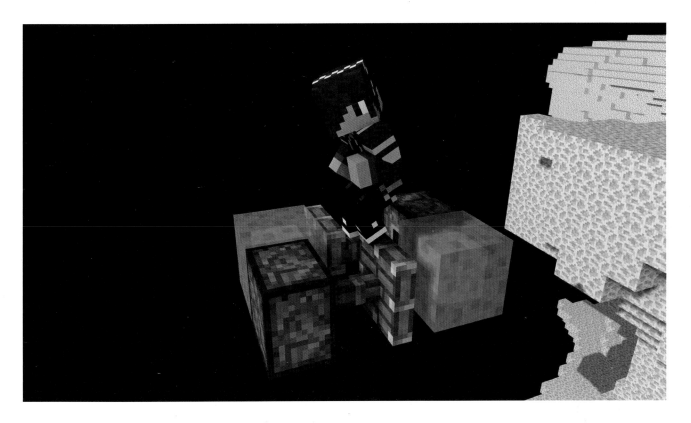

build your contraption and set off for the outer islands. You can use an invisibility potion to minimize the chance the dragon will see you, and sneaking can increase the distance at which the dragon will notice you. It may take you about ten minutes or so to either fly or bridge over to an Outer Island. Once there, arm and armor yourself with enchanted gear and go in seek of chorus plants, End cities, shulkers, End city ships, and the Elytra. Once you've gathered your loot, place it safely in the Ender chest you've brought. You'll have to die to return to the Overworld and only an Ender chest will preserve your goodies.

END, BUILD YOUR HOME IN THE

SSP, Gameplay, Building

Can you transform an island or island city in the end into a place to call your own? Even if you can't sleep in the End, you should be able to make a pretty interesting life there. The only things standing in your way are the Endermen, some shulkers . . . and the Dragon.

ETERNAL NIGHT CHALLENGE

SSP, Gameplay

How long can you survive in an endless night? In this community challenge proposed by Maximux12 on Minecraftforum.net, you'll have to create your survival world with cheats on. Once you spawn, you have one day to collect resources. When it becomes dark at night, type in the command /gamerule doDaylightCycle false. To keep things extra scary, you can make sure your brightness level is set at Moody. For more challenges, add in a rule that beds aren't allowed or play in hardcore mode!

ETHO'S SPEED CHALLENGES, COMPETE WITH

SSP, Competition

Etho is a very popular Minecraft YouTuber known for his technical builds, inventiveness,

excellent videos and commentary, and dry sense of humor. Some years ago, along with help from his viewers, he created a unique set of fun speed challenges, and the overall rules are:

- Create a new world use a random seed, with structures turned off (except where mentioned), and set to hardcore mode
- No use of F3
- No use of beds
- Try to accomplish the challenges in thirty minutes

Etho himself rarely completed any of these within thirty minutes; most took between thirty-five and forty minutes. You can see videos of the challenges on his YouTube channel, EthosLab.

The Etho Minecraft Speed Challenges are:

1. **Kill a Ghast:** Get to the Nether and kill one ghast.
2. **Play a Record:** The record must be the

one that is dropped by a creeper shot by a skeleton.

3. **Five-Course Meal:** Make a cooked porkchop, cooked fish, bread, mushroom stew, and a cake.

4. **The Color Wheel:** Create all sixteen colors of wool. You can take colored wool from the sheep or dye the wool.

5. **Companions:** Tame a wolf and a cat, craft an iron and a snow golem, and get them all in the same location.

6. **Brew Master:** (Leave structures on.) Make all the main types of potion brewable in-game in one hour. You don't need to make potions altered by secondary ingredients like glowstone, redstone, gunpowder, dragon's breath, or fermented spider eye. For Java Edition 1.12, this means ten potions: Night Vision, Fire Resistance, Leaping, Swiftness, Water Breathing, Healing, Poison, Regeneration, Strength, and Weakness.

7. **Treasure Hunter:** (Leave structures on.) You have thirty minutes to collect as many treasure chests as you can from dungeons, villages, mineshafts, strongholds, temples, and Nether fortresses.

8. **Hungry Man:** (Leave structures on.) Get as many unique food items as possible. Each unique food item counts as one point. Cooked and uncooked meat are separate items, and golden apples and carrots are also included in the list.

9. **XP Madness:** (No visiting the Nether.) Get as much XP as you can within thirty minutes.

EVERYTHING, GET

SSP, Quest, Competition

This Get-Everything-in-Minecraft challenge has been a staple challenge pretty much since the beginning of Minecraft. It keeps getting harder with each new version, as Mojang adds more stuff and more blocks. That doesn't stop it from being fun though. As a personal challenge, you can take your time to get literally one of everything possible in survival Minecraft: every block and every item, from andesite to zombie flesh. Or you can give yourself (and any other participants in a group challenge) a time limit, and award one point for every item or block you get during the competition.

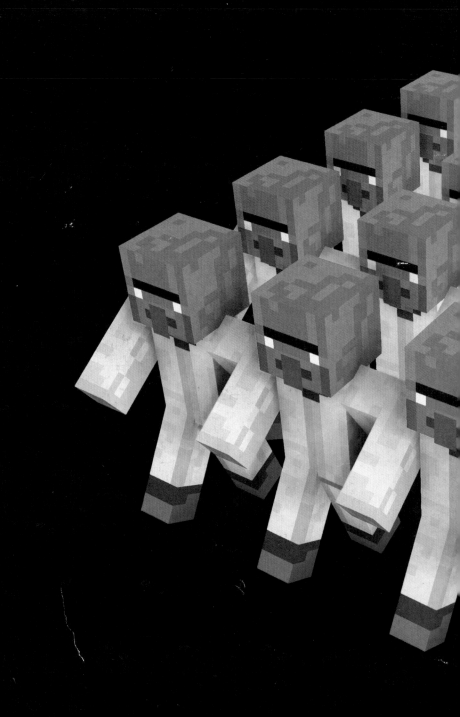

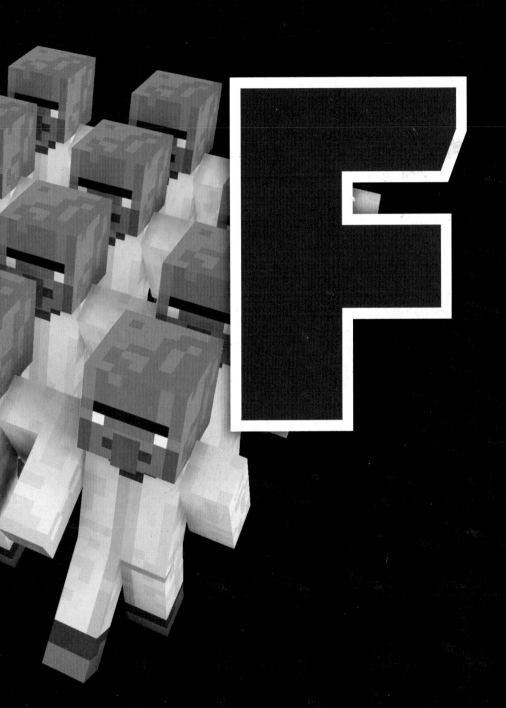

F

FACTIONS SERVER, PLAY ON A

SMP, Server, Gameplay

Factions are another organized gameplay type popular on multiplayer servers. They're geared toward PvP, primarily between teams of players called factions. When you join a server, you can start off alone and form your own faction (not recommended for new players) or join an existing faction. The best experience is probably had if you join with a few friends, simply because of the heavy emphasis on PvP and destruction. The goal of each faction is to control as much land on the server as possible, conquer and claim other faction's bases, and maintain power by increasing the faction size and dying as little as possible.

Popular factions servers include Desteria.com, TheArchon.net, and Snapcraft.net.

FAR LANDS, VISIT THE

SSP, Quest

In very early versions of Minecraft (before beta 1.8), the algorithm for generating infinite terrain had a few glitches. If you got out really far from spawn, over twelve and a half million blocks away, the Minecraft world started to break down. There would be flooding, unexplained darkness, giant walled borders, and

spooky strange terrain generation. You would also experience glitches, stuttering, and jumps in gameplay as well. To find out more about the Far Lands, visit the official wiki at Minecraft.gamepedia.com, which also includes information on various ways to make it to the Far Lands yourself.

Minecraft YouTuber Kurt J. Mac has made it his mission (for the Child's Play charity), as well as a name for himself and an entry in the Guinness World Records, to walk to the Far Lands. You can jump into his adventure at any point easily in his YouTube series, Far Lands or Bust.

One of the easiest ways to view the Far Lands for yourself is to use an NBT editor to transport yourself in a beta version of Minecraft. First, create a world using a historical beta version of Minecraft: beta 1.7. Once you create the world, open and close it. There's no creative mode or commands in this version, so you have to move yourself the 12.5 million blocks by editing the actual data in the game. To do this, you'll need to open up the beta 1.7 world's level.dat file (Be very, very careful that you are selecting the right file in the right world!) in an NBT editor. NBT is the name of the type of file used in Minecraft for storing data. You can find an online NBT editor at https://irath96.github.io/webNBT. You can drag and drop your level.dat file here. Then, you need to look for the Player entries, and in these the Pos (position) entries. The Pos entries 0, 1, and 2 stand for your X, Y, and Z coordinates. Change both 0 and 2 to 12550750. Change 1 to 75. (1 is the height you'll be at, and you want to avoid suffocating in a hill.) Finally, save the edited level.dat file. Replace the level.dat file in your Far Lands world folder with the new edited one. Open up Minecraft beta 1.7

In this online NBT editor, you drop your level.dat file that defines your world, and then you can search for and change data settings. Here, the position 0 (X-coordinate setting) for Player is highlighted. You need to be very careful when editing NBT values, as this kind of manipulation can corrupt your game.

again and your world, and you should be about a hundred or so blocks from the Far Lands. (If you do find yourself in a hill and can't punch your way out, re-edit the level.dat file so that your y coordinate is higher.) The game will probably be very jumpy as you move, but press on, and you should be able to reach this famous terrain.

FICTIONAL BUILDING, BRING TO LIFE A FAVORITE

SSP, Building

Reconstruct a special building or buildings from a book, comic, or film you've loved. The Secret Garden in the book of the same name by Frances Hodgson Burnett, Laura Ingalls Wilder's cabin from *Little House on the Prairie*, Batman's bat cave, Superman's Fortress of Solitude, the Hobbit dwellings of Lord of the Rings are just a few fictional buildings that can be recreated.

FIREWORKS SHOW, PUT ON A

SSP, Quest

Minecraft includes variety of firework shapes, colors, and sizes, and you can easily make an impressive timed firework show. You can

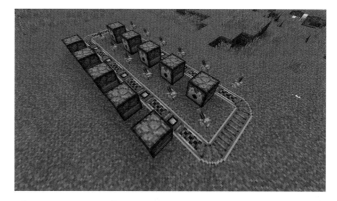

There are several ways to automate setting off fireworks. Here, activator rails beside dispensers will activate the dispensers when a minecart goes by.

manually set the fireworks off in sequence, set up a random show with a dispenser, or use redstone to time each burst. To make a fireworks rocket, you'll need to first craft a fireworks star and then use that to craft the rocket.

A fireworks star can be crafted with gunpowder and, in the other eight slots of a crafting table, up to eight different dye, zero to one shape effect items, and zero to two special effects items. Shape effects items include fire charge (larger sphere), gold nugget (star shape), mob head (creeper head shape), and feather (burst). Special effects items are: glowstone dust (twinkling) and diamond (trailer).

You can also add a colored fade effect by crafting a finished firework star with one dye.

Finally, to make the rockets, craft a firework star with one paper and one to three gunpowder—the more gunpowder, the longer the firework will travel before exploding.

If you want to create fireworks with command blocks, there are online command generators that allow you to pick the colors, shapes, and effects for a firework and will give you the command for crafting the rocket(s).

FLASH MOB, STAGE A

SMP, Server, Quest

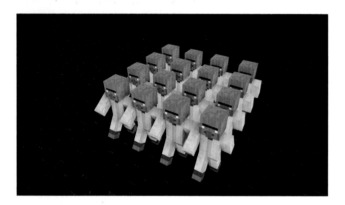

A flash mob is an event where a group of people gather unexpectedly (to others) in a public space and perform an unusual activity; in real life, this is often a dance to recorded music. A flash mob is meant to surprise people and entertain them. You can see videos of flash mobs online. You can also do this in Minecraft! You can gather with a group of friends on a public or shared server. At the same time, everyone performs the same action, like jumping, sprint jumping in a tango line, dancing—it's up to you. For an even bigger effect, wear the same skin or a set of obviously matching skins. You can also find

videos of Minecraft player flash mobs on YouTube, like the ones created by OfficialLemon-Cats, Critical, Tinotria (German), and SumatraDIG (French).

THE FLOOR IS LAVA, PLAY

SSP, Map

In the real world, to play "The Floor Is Lava," everyone pretends the floor is lava and jumps to the nearest safe place, like a chair or table. In a Minecraft "The Floor Is Lava" challenge, the floor can actually be lava! There are more than a few ways to set this game up. You could make a parkour-style mini-game yourself, featuring lava as the bottom surface. Or you can use a world editor to add a top layer of lava to a part of your world. Probably the easiest way is to play one of the many downloadable Floor Is Lava maps: Among others, there's "The Floor Is Lava Map" by BrendenMC, "Lava Floor" by

Penguin2598, and "The Floor is Lava 1.12" by AryFireZ.

FOSSILS, FIND AND EXCAVATE ALL THE TYPES OF

SSP, Quest

Find each of the Minecraft fossil structures, excavating and exposing them to view from ground level. If you're not in a race, add some archaeologist's huts!

There are eight types of fossil structures in Minecraft: four head structures and four spine structures. They're large structures, up to about five blocks high and fourteen long, all made of the bone block, although a block here or there in the structure may be replaced with a block of coal ore. This is presumably because the bone block has degraded further into fossil charcoal. You'll find the fossils buried (not too deeply, typically between y=40 and y=50) in deserts and swamps.

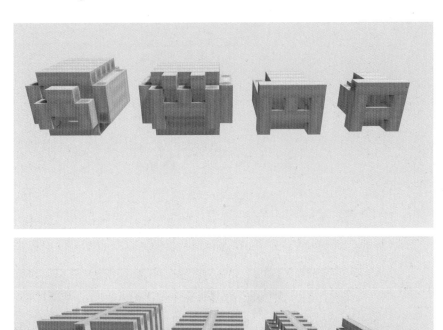

There are four types of fossilized skulls and four types of fossilized spines to find.

GEOLOGIST, BE THE

SSP, Quest

The Minecraft game uses a special randomized world generator to create the infinite and unique worlds you play in. The algorithm for generating the terrain includes specifications on where to randomly generate features like caves, lava pools, mountains, lakes, rivers, and more. Play the geologist, exploring and discovering your world: find, document, and take a screenshot of every type of natural world structure (not including biomes and buildings). These natural structures include mountains (with sheer, unclimbable faces) and hills (smaller, with all sides climbable sides), floating islands, overhangs, hollows (where many overhangs overlap), oceans, lakes, lava lakes below- and aboveground, rivers, beaches, basins (an area with exposed stone), icebergs, and ravines. Document the types of caves and caverns that you find. Types include:

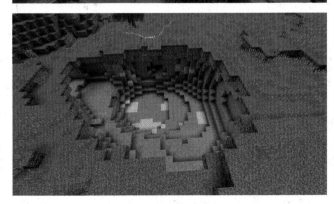

Three unusual types of formations to look out for: basins, caverns, and hollows.

- Shallow, small caves near the surface
- Circular caverns open to the sky
- Large, spherical caverns underground
- Giant entrances like an open cylinder descending almost straight down.

GHAST, CATCH, NAME, AND TRANSPORT A

SMP, Quest

Even if you're not planning on getting all the in-game advancements, catching a ghast and bringing it to the Overworld is a real badge of honor. Ghasts need a 4-block high area to spawn, at any light level, and not in a Nether fortress. You'll want to carve out a large platform that is only four blocks high (netherrack above and below), with room for a ghast to spawn twenty-four blocks away from you. Try to eliminate other spawnable areas nearby. When they spawn, their legs will be in the netherrack beneath, and they won't be able to move, though they can rotate a bit. They can still see you and blast you. However, you can race to get close, enclose it to prevent it from shooting

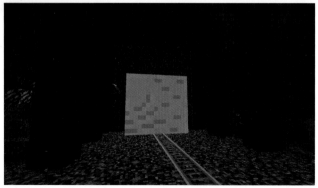

Once a ghast is captured in a minecart, it is centered above the minecart and can be rolled on rails to your oversized portal.

you, and name it so it won't despawn. Hazards include suffocating the ghast and difficulties stopping and restarting the minecart with the ghast in it. Stay out of the ghast's sightline (comes from a point between its eyes), and blinker the ghast by placing blocks at its eye level so it can't see you. To see (and turn off) hitboxes and sightlines, toggle F3 and B. You'll also need a portal big enough for the ghast to fit through. Once you get the ghast in the minecart to the portal, you'll have to get it out of the minecart and push it through the portal. The Overworld side of the portal should be fitted with a minecart and rails and a contained area.

This challenge is best performed with friends. If you're running into problems, open a Creative world and run through your plan to troubleshoot. For an entertaining, real-time look at some very funny YouTubers accomplishing this task, look on YouTube for Tango Tek and impulseSV's three-hour live stream replay from March 24, 2016.

GIANT, BUILD SOMETHING

SSP, Building

Build something giant. Use Minecraft itself as your inspiration—build a giant chest, a towering sword, or a massive creeper!

GUINNESS WORLD RECORD, BEAT A MINECRAFT

SSP, Competition

The Guinness World Records actually includes feats accomplished in Minecraft! From the Longest Tunnel Created in Minecraft (100,000 blocks long) to the Fastest Time to Build a Minecraft House (3:54), there are over 150 total world records involving Minecraft. To view all of these, you'll need to sign up for an account and use their advanced record search. Some records are still open to be broken, and you can apply to enter your record. You can also apply to request a new achievement to be a world record. Go to Guinessworldrecords.com and search for Minecraft to get started.

GUINNESS CHALLENGES, TAKE ON A

SSP, Competition

In 2015, Guinness World Records set up a series of timed challenges for Minecraft players to compete in. Although the challenge contest ended in 2016, the challenges themselves are fun, short challenges. See the specific rules for each challenge on its web page at Guinessworldrecords.com/challengers/minecraft. Here you can also see the times and videos of the original challenge contestants. Compete with your friends on these tasks or use them as inspiration for your own set of challenges.

- Fastest time to kill ten zombie pigmen
- Fastest time to dig to bedrock
- Fastest time to craft all ten Minecraft tools
- Fastest time to build an iron golem
- Fastest time to build a house
- Tallest staircase built in one minute
- Most wood collected in three minutes
- Fastest time to build a two-block piston door

In this challenge description, you start off with sixty-four coal, sixty-four stone, one pumpkin, thirty-six iron ore, and four wooden planks in a Superflat, peaceful world. You can use only these items to create the resources you need to craft the golem.

HARDCORE CHALLENGE

SSP, Gameplay

Minecraft makes it relatively painless to get over an in-game death. You're teleported back to your spawn location, and your base and builds are all still there. Unless you died in lava or the ocean or lost somewhere, you have a good chance of getting back to your point of death and retrieving your goods. For a goose-pimply challenge, get out of easy, normal, or hard mode and switch to hardcore. Hardcore is hard mode plus, and the plus means permanent death and deletion of your world if you die. No going back. It will change the way you step out of your cozy home in the morning, how late you stay out at night, and the value of enchanted diamond weapons and armor.

If you're committed to extensive base building, and losing a world would cause you untold grief, use hardcore game mode to test yourself at shorter challenges. For example, how many hardcore deaths and worlds does it take you to reach the Nether, or reach the End, or find an Elytra?

In hardcore mode, you get one life. When you die, your world is deleted.

HEAD HUNTER

SSP, Quest

Based on an old, early Minecraft achievement, this challenge demands that you acquire the heads of a zombie, skeleton, wither skeleton, and creeper. You'll have to either capture, manage, or create a charged creeper and incite it to explode, killing your prey. From acquiring the charged creeper to timing its explosion without dying yourself, this is one of the most difficult things to accomplish in Minecraft.

HERMIT CHALLENGE

SSP, Gameplay

The Hermit Challenge is a classic gameplay challenge that players often play with their own rules and restrictions. However, the main restriction is that you'll be spending your life hiding away from others and/or the Overworld by living your entire life underground, never coming up for light. You can spend one first day aboveground, but at night you'll have to retreat underground. From then on, you'll have to get your wood from abandoned mineshafts or underground tree farms and set up food farms below the surface, so gather as many seeds and saplings as possible!

You'll be spending your game life underground in this challenge, so you may want to make it cozy!

HISTORICAL, REAL-LIFE, OR TRADITIONAL BUILDING, BUILD A

SSP, Building

Build a famous, historical, or traditional building from the real world. You don't have to build the Louvre or the Taj Mahal. There are many fascinating and beautiful traditional building styles, even ordinary and charming homes,

Minecrafter and educator Momibelle (@MCKidsAcademy) built this reproduction of a traditional Berber village in the Atlas Mountains of Morocco.

that are relatively easy to build. Building villages or homes in traditional styles that you'll find in different cultures is a great way to travel around the world in Minecraft. Research a building or building style you find interesting, and you'll find out more about the people who lived in them as well as learn how to translate these styles into Minecraft. For some samples, you can Google "traditional building" and "vernacular architecture." Vernacular architecture is a term architects use to describe buildings that belong to a specific culture, group, geographical location, or time. They are ordinary, informal buildings built by local people in styles that continue through generations, styles and functions suited to their locale, culture, and climate.

- Berber villages in the Atlas Mountains
- Mongolian nomad yurt or ger camps
- Inuit igloos
- Log cabins of North America
- Fujian tulou of China
- Viking longhouses
- Cliff dwellings of the American southwest

HISTORY OF MINECRAFT, DISCOVER THE

OOG

Minecraft is the second best-selling game of all time, after Tetris. Why is it so popular? Who made it? There are a few books about the subject that you can read to become an expert on all the activity behind the scenes, so head to the library. In addition to these books about the development of Minecraft, you'll also pick up tidbits of historical information from the development company Mojang's other guides and books, as well as the official Minecraft website at Minecraft.net.

Minecraft, Second Edition: The Unlikely Tale of Markus "Notch" Persson and the Game That Changed Everything by Daniel Goldberg (2015, Seven Stories Press), 304 pp.

A Year with Minecraft: Behind the Scenes at Mojang by Thomas Arnroth (2014, ECW Press), 216 pp.

For children:

Minecraft Creator Markus Notch Persson by Kari Cornell (2016, Lerner Classroom.) 32 pp. Ages 7–11.

The Inventors of Minecraft: Markus Notch Persson and His Coding Team by Jill Keppeler (2017, Powerkids pr) 32 pp. Ages 8–11.

HOBO CHALLENGE

SSP, Gameplay

Like the Hermit Challenge, this is a classic gameplay challenge that has had many variations over the years for different players. Survive in Minecraft for thirty Minecraft days and nights without living in a house or sleeping in a bed. You don't have a chest to hold things in, and you never spend a night in the same place twice. You can, however, take shelter in a village, for just one night per village. Oh, and there's another catch. You can't use F3 or a map, so you'll need to get good at finding your way around!

Variation: Start your hobo world with a small starter house. Store all your belongings in the house, then set off for seven days as a hobo. At the end of the seven days, try to find your way back home. Play on hardcore mode!

HOW DID WE GET HERE?

Advancement

To get this super challenging advancement in Minecraft, you'll need to experience all status effects available in Survival mode at the same time. This includes all potion effects, beacon effects, and effects from mobs!

The current full list for Java Edition 1.12.2 is Absorption, Fire Resistance, Glowing, Haste, Hunger, Invisibility, Jump Boost, Levitation, Mining Fatigue, Nausea, Night Vision, Poison, Regeneration, Resistance, Slowness, Speed, Strength, Water Breathing, Weakness, and Wither. You'll want to wait to attempt this until you've killed the End dragon and a wither and you have a beacon and Elytra wings.

Winning tactics include planning out the sequence of effect getting; maximizing the duration of effects to allow you more time to get the rest of the effects; minimizing the time spent between getting the effects (drinking potions, etc.); using dispensers to apply multiple splash potions and arrows; using mining carts and boats and Nether portals to transport mobs; using tags to name mobs so they won't despawn; and making sure you are hungry so you'll be able to eat any food needed for effects. This challenge is much easier done with friends, but it is possible by yourself. For inspiration and tips, look on YouTube for videos from other players attempting this challenge.

INVOLVED IN THE COMMUNITY, GET

OOG

Whether you are a new player or a pro, there are thousands of communities and millions of players not too different from you. Get involved in a community that appeals to you, whether it's a multiplayer server with features you like or a forum where you can ask and answer questions and share your creations.

Planetminecraft.com is a popular destination for players, and you can share screenshots, projects, blog posts, mods, and more. The Official Minecraft forum is at Minecraftforum.net. There are lists of family-friendly multiplayer servers to join—just search "family-friendly Minecraft servers" or "kid-friendly Minecraft servers" to get started.

Another way to get involved is through contributing to the Minecraft game and development world by helping modders and modpack creators by beta testing, becoming a moderator at a server, and supporting modders, streamers, and other content developers. Many content creators and modders have Patreon sites; typically, for a $10 monthly fee you can join their server and discussion groups. You may also want to make a mod yourself! Also, look locally: there may be groups of Minecrafters who gather at a library or other meeting place and play on a local network together.

IRON MAN AND OTHER COLLECTION RACES

SSP, SMP, Competition

In this challenge posted by Neoxx on the Minecraftforum.net, you race to get every single item that uses iron in its recipe. No strip mining is allowed, and you must play in hardcore mode: one life only. You can use the idea of this challenge as a way to create variations: race to collect all items of a particular type or items found in a particular biome. For example, collect all horse armor or all flower types.

See also: Scavenger hunts
All Items Made with Iron

JURASSICCRAFT MOD, LIVE WITH DINOSAURS WITH THE

SSP, SMP, Mod

Your computer may not be powerful enough to handle the hundred-mod modpacks that are the most popular, but this doesn't have to stop

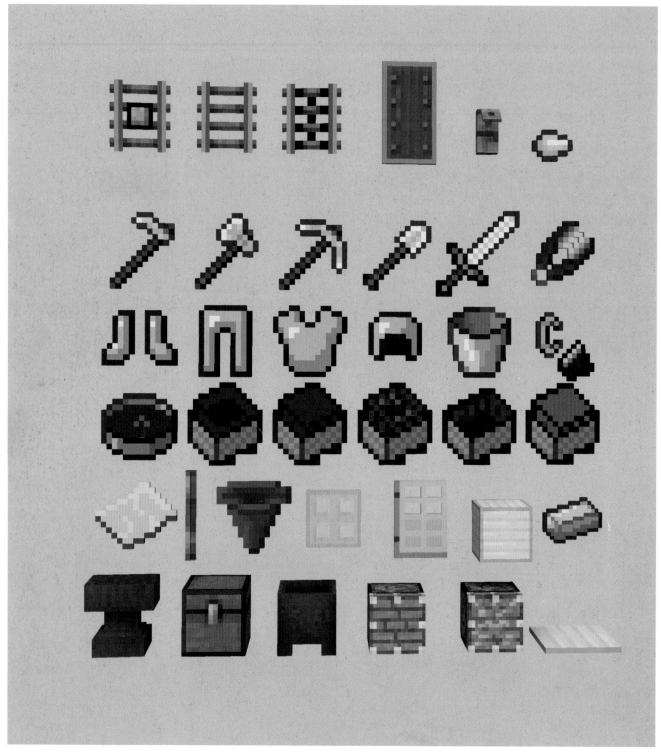

In the Iron Man challenge, you must find or craft every item that uses iron.

you from enjoying playing with mods. You can play with one or two mods at a time, using the third-party Minecraft launcher called MultiMC. You can also create a custom profile with the Twitch launcher and install just one mod at a time. If you're ready, one mod you should definitely check out is JurassiCraft2. It lets you gather ancient DNA and bring dinosaurs to life for your very own Jurassic Park–style adventure! The dinosaur and skeleton models are amazing.

There is a public server you can join if you download the Official JurassiCraft Modpack on the Twitch launcher. You can find out more about the mod at its wiki (jurassicraftmod.wikia.com) and from YouTube videos.

These Brachiosauruses are just two of the stunning dinosaurs in the JurassiCraft mod.

KING OF THE LADDER

SMP, Mini-Game

A simple but hugely entertaining game, King of the Ladder was invented by popular YouTubers Etho, Nebris, VintageBeef, and W92Baj while they played together on the private Mindcrack server. To play, build a pillar up as high as you like, with ladders on each side. The first person to the top or who can stay at top for a set amount of time (one to five minutes or so) is king. Rules: you can't break the column or the ladder. In different variations, weapons to help knock other players off are allowed. You can place a pool of water at the bottom to prevent deaths, or not to allow deaths. In the latter case, players will want beds nearby to set their spawn so they can keep on playing. To see the original hijinks of the first King of the Ladder game, search YouTube for "Etho Mindcrack SMP – Episode 10: King of the Ladder."

KINGDOM, BUILD YOUR OWN

SSP, Building

Why stop at a city or base? Build your own kingdom—with villages, castles, farms, and roads. Set a theme for your kingdom (dwarven, steampunk, medieval, fairy). Have different themes

This simple yet endlessly entertaining mini-game is easy to construct.

for different villages, or have different areas produce different Minecraft resources. For inspiration, watch YouTuber BdoubleO100's Building with Bdouble0 season 2 (pt 2) series, in which he constructs a world of several kingdoms, each with a different theme and backstory. You can even download his world to tour and play.

LOOTING CHALLENGE

SSP, Gameplay

In this challenge, everything you get must be through looting! You're averse to working, farming, chopping, shearing, mining, and contraption building. Fishing for treasure and junk is fine. Find enough wild sugarcane to trade paper with villagers and fish for your food, and explore your world. Loot villages, temples, and pirate ships. If you acquire a pick or ax, you can use it to loot blocks from walls, floors, and roofs, or force your way into a structure. You can also use a sword or bow against mobs. You'll be on the lookout for abandoned mineshafts, buried treasure, jungle and desert temples, woodland mansions, villages, strongholds, dungeons, igloos, underwater ruins, Nether

fortresses, and more. Your goal is to make it to the Nether and to an End city to acquire the rare Elytra. To advance to the Nether, you'll have to either build a Nether portal using just a bucket, water, and lava or find obsidian in villages. Set it alight with fire, and you're in.

LUCKY BLOCK MOD, PLAY

SSP, SMP, Mod

The incredibly popular Lucky Block mod adds just one block to your Minecraft world. The Lucky Block spawns randomly, although you can craft it with your otherwise fairly useless gold ingots. Break the lucky block and you might get some great loot (a collection of potions, an enchanting table), or something bad might happen (a deadly explosion or a powerful zombie). You can also craft especially lucky or unlucky Lucky Blocks. Use the Twitch launcher or the MultiMC launcher to play with this mod, but make sure you are in a world you don't mind destroying!

See also: MultiMC, Twitch Launcher

In a world modded with Lucky Block, you will occasionally find lucky blocks in custom builds like this around the map.

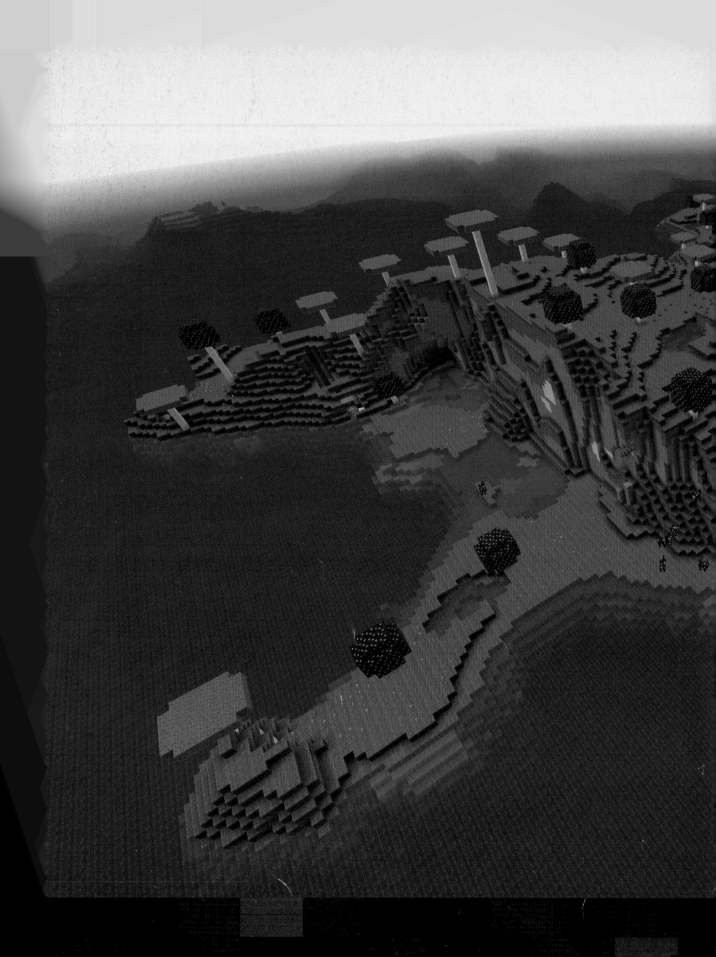

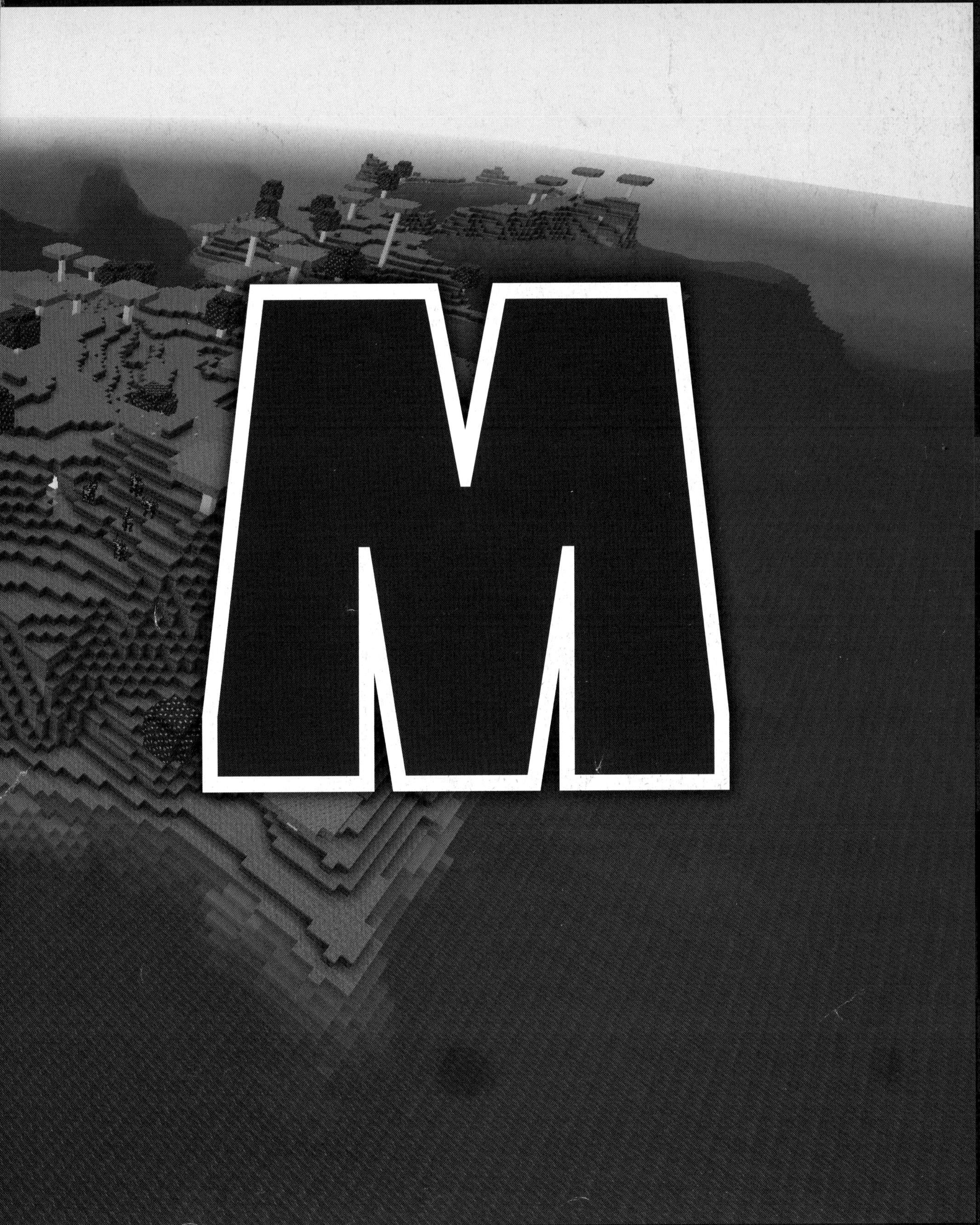
M

MAP ART, MAKE

SSP, Quest

In addition to making pixel art using Minecraft blocks, you can also create map art. To do this, you place blocks on flattened ground to make a horizontal picture. Then you use an in-game map to map it. To make sure you have the framing right on your picture, make the map that will "hold" the final picture first. Once you've set this up, level the area that the map covers. Make a border so you can see exactly where the edges of the map are. Finally make your picture on the ground, one block at a time.

Map art is basically horizontal pixel art. However, unlike pixel art, you can use a technique of placing some blocks higher than ground level to change how light and dark their colors appear in the final map. A Minecraft map shows blocks at higher elevations as lighter, so you can use a white block at different levels to create shades of light gray.

You do have a limited number of colors to use in your map art. Minecraft maps use a limited number of colors, and each of these

This map was made with a photo of the moon and converted to a map using djfun's map making tool, MC Map Item Tool at http://mc-map.djfun.de.

colors is made by one or by several different blocks. For example, the map will show the same light blue color whether you use a block of diamond, prismarine bricks, or dark prismarine. On the other hand, a light to middle green is only created by a grass block. You can see a list of map colors that are available and the blocks that make them on the official Minecraft wiki at Minecraft.gamepedia.com/Map_item_format.

See also: Pixel Art.

MAPS, PLAY A BUNCH OF

SSP, SMP, Maps

Maps are free, game-within-a-game worlds created by other users for you to play on. They usually have a limited world area or world borders, so they are much smaller overall than the essentially infinite survival Minecraft world.

There are hundreds, if not thousands, of Minecraft maps to play and many different types of maps too. In general, maps are categorized as Adventure (for exploring and battling), Creative (featuring creative builds, often cities, to explore), Horror (scary!), Parkour (jumping over and around obstacles), Puzzle (puzzles to solve in order to advance through levels), and

Survival (the mapmakers will usually make it a bit harder to survive than in normal Minecraft). You may also see the category CTM (Complete the Monument) or Race for the Wool. In these, you typically battle through a landscape, exploring every nook and cranny to find every color of wool and place each color on a monument that keeps track of your progress.

Some maps are so amazingly detailed, balanced, and fun that you'll find many videos of them on YouTube. If you want to explore all that Minecraft has to offer, you need to check out at least a few of these amazing maps. You can find maps online at many websites; a few of the most popular map sites are Minecraftforum.net, Minecraftmaps.com, Planetminecraft.com, and Hypixel.net (under Forums >Hypixel Community>Official Hypixel Maps).

To play a map on Java Edition, you'll need to download the map (world) file, placing it in the correct folder in your Minecraft game files. You must open the world with the right version of Minecraft. Check the description of the map from the download site to make sure you follow all instructions. On Bedrock Edition, you can download maps through the Store.

See also: Creative Maps, Dropper, SkyBlock, Survival Island

One of the most popular and downloaded maps is the Assassin's Creep parkour map created by Selib and DrChriz and inspired by the Assassin's Creed video game.

MAZE, BUILD A

SMP, Quest, Building

This maze pattern was generated by Jamis Buck's Minecraft Maze Generator at Jamisbuck.org/mazes/minecraft.html.

Create a hedge maze for your friends to puzzle or race through. Plan the maze out on paper first, then use leaf blocks to create the hedges. Add a prize for the first to reach the end. In the same manner, you could create a dangerous maze with wrong turns that lead to traps, a flat maze made simply of path blocks, or an underground labyrinth to escape from. If you don't want to spend the time figuring out a maze pattern, you can use an online maze generator.

MCMMO, PLAY MINECRAFT RPG STYLE WITH

SMP, Gameplay, Modded

MCMMO is a popular plug-in feature on multiplayer servers. It adds in an RPG-like skill system element to Minecraft. Skills measured include acrobatics, archery, axes, excavation, fishing, herbalism, mining, repair, smelting, swords, taming, unarmed, and woodcutting. As you perform actions associated with each skill, you gain experience. When your experience at a skill reaches certain levels, you'll be given special bonuses, like rare drops or speedier results. You'll find it on servers that incorporate other RPG elements, like Factions servers.

On the left of the screen, you can see the categories of skills you can level up in.

MEDIEVAL VILLAGE, BUILD A

SSP, Building

It's a popular build challenge, but it is a goodie. The log, planks, bricks, and building blocks in Minecraft seem perfectly suited to recreating villages from medieval Europe. There's also lots of inspiration online, where you can find examples of other players builds on popular Minecraft forums and Pinterest, as well as videos and instructions on YouTube. Different buildings you may want to include in your village are a town hall, an inn, a blacksmith, a bakery, a mill, a woodcutter's, a well, farms, homes, stables, and shops. Planning ahead always helps. You can list the buildings you want in your village, plan roads, and locate where your buildings should go. When you're done, you can populate your village with Minecraft villagers!

MINECOLONIES MOD, PLAY THE

SSP, SMP, Modded

On the list of full-featured, pretty much standalone mods that really extend Minecraft's gameplay is the MineColonies mod. With it, you establish a town hall, bring in colonists, and assign a builder. Task the builder with the job of building various worker huts (fisher, farmer, miner, etc.) and then you can assign the colonists jobs. The builder will need to make the colonists homes, too, to sleep in and increase their happiness levels. And you'll need a warehouse, food for the colonists, along with some guards to battle against the enemy barbarians, who will wipe you out if you are not careful. If you are looking for a really different gameplay experience in Minecraft and you like building towns, this may be the one mod for you. A helpful community, wiki, and more information is at Minecolonies.com. You can also play this mod as a part of several modpacks, including the MineColonies Official modpack, on the Twitch launcher.

With the MineColonies mod, you can create a colony filled with miners, loggers, farmers, guards, warehouses, and more—all with working citizens!

MINI-GAMES, TRY A FEW

SMP, Server, mini-games

Mini-games are games played inside Minecraft. Typically they are short games you play with others on a server. There are many different kinds of games—take-offs of the Hunger Games, building games, jump-on-the-right-block games, hide-and-seek games, and more. Multiplayer mini-game servers offer dozens of games that start around the clock for you to join in. Server lobbies (where you spawn in) will guide you to different game areas, which usually feature a short tutorial. Popular mini-games servers include Mineplex.com, Hypixel.com, and Hivemc.com.

MINI GOLF COURSE, BUILD AND PLAY

SSP, SMP, Competition

In Minecraft mini golf, you toss a golf ball (any item like a snowball or slime ball) on a surface made of ice or, better yet, packed ice. (Packed ice doesn't melt if a torch is nearby.) The slipperiness of the ice lets the item slide along toward your goal. You can make your Putt-Putt course with holes to slide the golfballs into and add obstacles, like narrow corridors, turns, and fences to make each hole different and a bit harder than a straight shot. If you are handy with redstone, you can even make moving obstacles!

Minecraft mini golf involves throwing an item onto ice to get it into the target area.

MODDING, LEARN

OOG, Modded, Skill

Mods to Minecraft (and other games) are made by players like yourself. While some mods change gameplay significantly, other mods are quite simple and may add only a few new blocks to the game. There are many resources to learn modding from, including books, websites, and video tutorials. Learning to mod will also get you on the path of learning to code and program! In addition, exploring the world of modding can introduce you to new communities of devoted modded Minecraft players, whether you decide to make a mod yourself or help other modders with beta testing.

MODPACK, MAKE YOUR OWN

SSP, Modded

You can very easily create your own custom modpack with the Twitch launcher. In the Mods/Minecraft page, click Create Custom Profile and select the version of Minecraft your modpack will use. Currently, the most recent version of Minecraft that modders are creating mods for is 1.12.2. The Twitch launcher will automatically select the right Forge version (a utility program that is a prerequisite for most mods). Click OK

to create your modpack profile. To add mods, click the large icon for your pack, and then click Get Mods. On the Mods page, you can browse and search for mods to add to your pack. Twitch will automatically only show you mods that are compatible with the version of Minecraft you selected. If you are just starting out playing with mods, or if your computer doesn't have a lot of RAM memory, you can install just one or two mods that you are interested in.

Twitch works in the background to prevent incompatibilities, but that doesn't mean you can't run into troubles with conflicting mods. In making your own modpack without technical support, and especially if you are just beginning to explore this world, it's often best to keep the number of mods you use to a minimum.

MODPACKS, PLAY A

SSP, SMP, Modded

Modpacks are selected bundles of mods designed to work well together. A modpack typically has a theme, even if the theme is "All the Mods!"

The easiest way to learn a modpack is to watch a YouTuber play a simple pack and follow along. Watch an episode, then recreate what they are doing in your own world. There are lots of YouTubers with different styles and sensibilities, so you should be able to find someone you enjoy watching. My personal favorite You-Tubers with Let's Play modded series are EthosLab, BdoubleO100, direwolf20, FalseSymmetry, GoodTimesWithScar, Java Vampire, and Mischief of Mice.

To start out your modded play, good packs include ones that come with a quest book. A quest book will give you quests to complete as you explore the mods in the modpack. A good quest book will guide you through the mods themselves, from easiest tasks to more difficult or dangerous tasks. A good modpack to start out with is (in 2018) Project Ozone Lite, which has a balanced quest book and which a number of popular YouTubers have played through.

See also: MultiMC, Twitch launcher

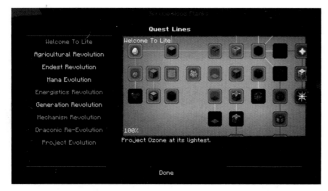

A quest book, like the one included with Project Ozone and Project Ozone Lite, can guide you through the different mods. Most quest books, like this, feature a set of categories, some ready to play and some locked. Locked categories can be unlocked by completing quests in other categories. Each category has a number of quests to complete. Here you can click on a quest icon to see what it entails.

MONSTER COLISEUM, BUILD A

SSP, Building

Some of the most pleasurable activities in Minecraft include bouncing, flying, exploding stuff, watching hostile mobs die in contraptions, and watching hostile mobs kill each other. I recommend building an arena, large or small, with the purpose of watching skeletons and other mobs fight each other in a battle royal. To get the mobs to fight each other, you'll want some skeletons, carefully and safely cordoned off in a position where they will try to hit you but instead fire at other mobs in the arena. Let the games begin!

MONSTERS HUNTED

Advancement

A Mooshroom Island is a fantastic place for your base: it's an island, it's free of hostile mobs, and if you can get rid of the mycelium and replant, the grass is as green as grass in the jungle.

To get this in-game advancement, you'll need to kill one of every type of hostile mob in the current version of Minecraft. Keep a checklist to help remember what's left. At present, the list is Blaze, Cave Spider, Creeper, Enderman, Evoker, Ghast, Guardian, Husk, Magma Cube, Phantom, Polar Bear, Shulker, Silverfish, Skeleton, Slime, Spider, Stray, Vindicator, Witch, Wither Skeleton, Zombie, Zombie Pigman, and Zombie Villager. Sharpen your swords!

MOOSHROOM ISLAND, FIND ONE AND BUILD YOUR BASE ON A

SSP, Gameplay

Mooshroom Islands are rare, but if you are one of the many who lean toward playing Peaceful difficulty because mobs make you jumpy, you can live a near stress-free life on the Mooshroom Island. No hostile mobs spawn on this island. Although the island is covered with mycelium—not the prettiest block in Minecraft—the biome itself supports a perfect, bright, green grass. To get this, you'll have to rid the island of mycelium and replace it with dirt. Ridding the island of mycelium isn't the easiest of chores because it spreads easily.

If you have trouble finding a Mooshroom Island, you can use the Minecraft tool Amidst or an online biome finder to search for one.

MULTIMC, ADD MODS WITH

SSP, OOG, Modded, Software

MultiMC is a custom Minecraft launcher that lets you create custom Minecraft profiles for modded or Vanilla play. You create a new instance, selecting the Vanilla version of Minecraft you want or a modpack from a list of FTB and other modpack organizations. If you select a Vanilla version, you can then edit that instance to add Forge and then any mods you download individually. If you regularly play different versions of Minecraft, Vanilla and/or modded, MultiMC is a great tool to keep your worlds and versions separate and manage your mods.

MULTIPLAYER, PLAY

SMP, Server

If you've never played on a multiplayer server, you should try this at least once. There are multiplayer servers geared toward younger players (family-friendly servers) and whitelist servers

In the New Instance page, you select the version of Minecraft you want.

that ask you a few questions before you're given access, usually to determine that you are the right age and enjoy the same play style. They'll also ask for your IGN to see if you've ever been banned from other servers. If you aren't quite ready to join a smaller server community, you can play mini-games with friends or by yourself on public servers like Hypixel, HiveMC, and Mineplex.

Gameplay style servers: There are some specific gameplay styles used on public servers. In Prison servers, you must mine your way to higher levels; in Economy servers, you compete to become the richest player. Factions servers pits groups of players against each other in a race to conquer bases and lands.

There are lists of these public servers at Minecraftservers.org, Minecraft-server-list.com,

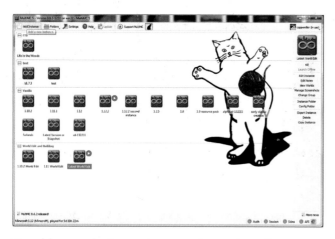

To add a new instance (a separate version of Minecraft), click Add Instance in the top menu. (Later, to add Forge [required for mods] and mods, click Edit Instance in the right toolbar.)

and Minecraft-mp.com, as well as smaller servers open for membership on Reddit. For family-friendly servers, search Google for "Minecraft family-friendly servers" or "Minecraft kid-friendly servers." Well-known family-friendly servers include Autcraft (for children on the autism spectrum), Cubeville, Famcraft, Intercraften, and Towncraft.

MUSIC, MAKE

SSP, Quest

You've probably swatted at a note block in Minecraft and heard the single tone, but did you know you can change the note they play and that they'll play a different instrument depending what block they are on ? And you can string them together to make a melody or even a song. Click the note block to make the sound, and right-click it one or more times to raise the note up to twenty-four semitones, or two full octaves including flats and sharps, starting at the default note of F# and going up to the second F# of the second octave. You can play a note by powering a block with redstone. This means you can

connect many blocks together with redstone, using repeaters to delay notes so they play in sequence. The default "instrument" of the note block is the harp (which sounds like a piano). For different instruments, place a note block on top of packed ice (chimes), wool (guitar), bone block (xylophone), clay (flute), or wood (double bass). For drum effects, use sand (snare drum), glass (clicks and sticks), or stone (bass drum).

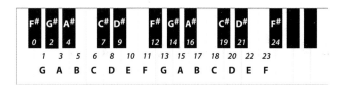

The note block goes two full octaves, as shown here. Each note has the number of right clicks you'll need to use on a note block to get to that note.

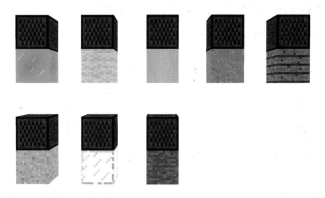

Place note blocks on different blocks to get the sounds of different instruments.

NAKED AND SCARED CHALLENGES, TRY IMPUSESV'S AND SKIZZLEMAN'S

SSP/SMP, Competition

Inspired by reality TV shows of survivalists battling elements in the wild, YouTubers and streamers impulseSV and Skizzleman have created a hilarious YouTube Minecraft challenge series called "Naked and Scared." (They actually wear undies.) Each season (an average of ten episodes), they're given a random challenge decided by their viewers. They must complete the challenge in twenty-one days in ultra hardcore mode along with abiding by other restrictions. As of now, the duo is up to fourteen seasons of hijinks, learning the hard way, and untimely deaths. Challenge yourself to see if you can accomplish the same feats, even if they weren't able to! And treat yourself to watching the series *and* the series official trailer.

Season 1: Obtain all sixteen colors of wool

Season 2: Locate one of each type of structure

Season 3: Kill a Wither boss

Season 4: Obtain a cobweb

Season 5: Catch and name a ghast

Season 6: Kill the Ender Dragon

Season 7: Kill three elder guardians

Season 8/9: Kill the Ender Dragon (New 1.9 fight)

Season 10: Name and trap one of each hostile mob

Season 11: Locate and conquer a Woodland mansion

Season 11.5 (live-streamed): Kill three elder guardians

Season 12: Complete the "How Did We Get Here?" advancement

Season 13: Get a ghast to shoot and kill three Overworld mobs

Season 14: Name and trap one of each hostile mob, like Season 10

NATURALIST PHOTOGRAPHER, BE A

SSP, Quest

Take a screenshot of every type of Minecraft creature—hostile, friendly, and neutral, young, and old. Check for new mobs added by the latest update, but currently the list includes:

Bat, Blaze, Cave spider, Chicken*, Chicken jockey, Cod, Cow*, Creeper, Dolphin, Donkey*, Drowned, Elder guardian, End Dragon, Enderman, Endermite, Evoker, Ghast, Guardian, Horse*, Husk, Iron golem, Llama*,

Magma cube, Mule (you'll need to breed these yourself!)*, Mooshroom*, Ocelot*, Parrot, Phantom, Pig*, Polar bear*, Pufferfish, Rabbit*, Salmon, Sheep*, Shulker, Silverfish, Skeleton*, Skeleton horse, Skeleton horseman, Slime, Snow golem, Spider, Spider jockey, Squid, Stray, Tropical fish[1]**, Turtle*, Vex, Vindicator, Witch, Wither, Wither skeleton, Wolf*, Zombie*, Zombie Pigman, Zombie Villager*.

You can use a photo editor's filters and border (on your computer or online to make your screenshots look like Polaroids or give them other effects.

---

1 There are twenty-two common varieties of tropical fish, but between combinations of two shapes, fifteen base colors, six patterns with fifteen colors, there are over 2,500 different variations. Get as many as you can!

NETHER HOME SWEET HOME

SSP, Gameplay

The title of this challenge says it all. You must make your home and farms in the Nether. You can bring in resources and animals from the Overworld, but you can't sleep in the Overworld. You'll have to do some planning to stop ghasts from ruining your abode!

NETHER HUB, BUILD A

SSP/SMP, Building

If you play in single-player worlds, a Nether hub can be a fantastic way to travel long distances and explore your never-ending world. That's because one block in the Nether is the same as traveling eight blocks in the same direction in the Overworld. If you play in multiplayer, a Nether hub is an essential way to travel to other people's bases and special locations (guardian temples, woodland mansions), and to return quickly to spawn. The Nether hub is a way to safely link up a bunch of Nether portals leading to these locations. You can use safe corridors, rail tracks, even boat-on-ice corridors to travel quickly between portals.

Building a Nether hub can be a long challenge but also a fun opportunity to show off your building skills. Not to mention your organization skills in planning the portal locations and paths, and know-how in keeping the hub safe from ghasts spawning inside it.

To translate Overworld coordinates to Nether equivalents, divide the Overworld x and z coordinates by 8 (y doesn't matter), and make sure to keep any negative values negative. One thing to remember is that a portal in the Nether will look for the closest active portal in the Overworld (within about 128 blocks), so if you haven't located an exact counterpart in the Overworld to a Nether portal in the Nether, it could link up to an existing portal. An easy way to prevent Nether portals crossing paths is to create the Overworld portal first but without going through it. Then create the Nether equivalent and go through this portal to confirm they have linked up.

This Nether hub uses glass, half slabs, and Nether wart to prevent ghasts from spawning.

NEVER SLEEP CHALLENGE

SSP, Gameplay

When Minecraft first came out, there were no beds and no sleeping. Today, a classic gameplay challenge is to return to the olden days: you can't sleep! Not only will mobs be spawning all night long around you, but you'll have to contend with the latest hostile mob that targets players low on sleep. Good luck and keep your eyes peeled for the phantoms in the sky!

NEXT GENERATION

Advancement

In this challenge, you'll need to get the dragon egg left after killing the dragon into your inventory. To do this, you can't just break the egg like you would a normal block, because it will teleport away and you could end up losing it over the edge of the end island. To get the egg to break as an item so you can pick it up, place a piston facing the egg. Activate the piston with a lever, and the egg will drop. Make sure to cover up portal blocks to prevent the egg from falling through. If for some reason the egg has teleported to a nearby location on an End stone, use the torch trick. This works because dragon eggs act like a sand block. Dig out a block two blocks below the egg and place a torch. Then break the block directly underneath the egg.

Use a piston to make the dragon egg block drop into an item you can pick up.

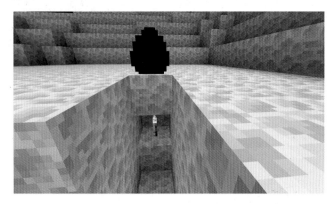

Here, when you break the End stone, the dragon egg will become an item when it falls on the candle.

The egg will fall on the torch and convert to an item, ready for you to claim.

NO ARMOR CHALLENGE

SSP, Gameplay

Another classic gameplay challenge is to play through your world with the restriction of wearing no armor. You can have all the weapons, tools, and shields you want, but no helmets, chest plates, leggings, or boots. Just like playing in hardcore mode, this will give you extra appreciation of your health and hunger! Up the ante by playing in hardcore mode, or ease up by allowing yourself to armor you've traded for with villagers.

NO CHESTS CHALLENGE

SSP, Gameplay

In this challenge, you cannot use any chest for any reason. Everything you have must be in your inventory or worn as armor. You'll have to

You have to get all your ores from caves and ravines in this challenge.

manage your inventory carefully and get rid of excess items by dropping them and letting them despawn. If you need extra temporary items in order to craft a new possession, you'll have to let some of your inventory rest on the ground and craft faster than they can despawn. For an even harder challenge, limit your possessions to the nine slots on your hotbar.

NO STRIP MINING

SSP, Gameplay

This challenge is perfect for players who, like me, tend to mine safely in strip mines, avoiding dark caves and mobs that hide there. It will get you out of your comfort zone and school you in the art of defending yourself while acquiring the coal, iron, and diamonds you need to advance. Try going down the caves with the goal of killing mobs, with mining ores as a reward when you clear and light an area.

NUCLEAR APOCALYPSE CHALLENGE

SSP, Gameplay

In this popular challenge of yore (posted by Dwarfdude194 in 2011), you must play as if you have just survived a nuclear apocalypse. Before the challenge begins, build an underground bunker and store these supplies: 10 wheat seeds, 5 bread, 16 torches, 1 stone pickax, 4 pumpkin seeds. You can also have any two of the following choices: 1 melon seed, 16 chicken eggs, 2 buckets of water, 1 cocoa bean and jungle sapling, 16 coal or charcoal. Head to your bunker to begin the challenge. From now on, you can't go outside unless fully armored, and the armor must be destroyed in an airlock before you return to your bunker. For additional rules and suggestions, visit the original post on the Minecraftforum. net (search for Nuclear Apocalypse Challenge).

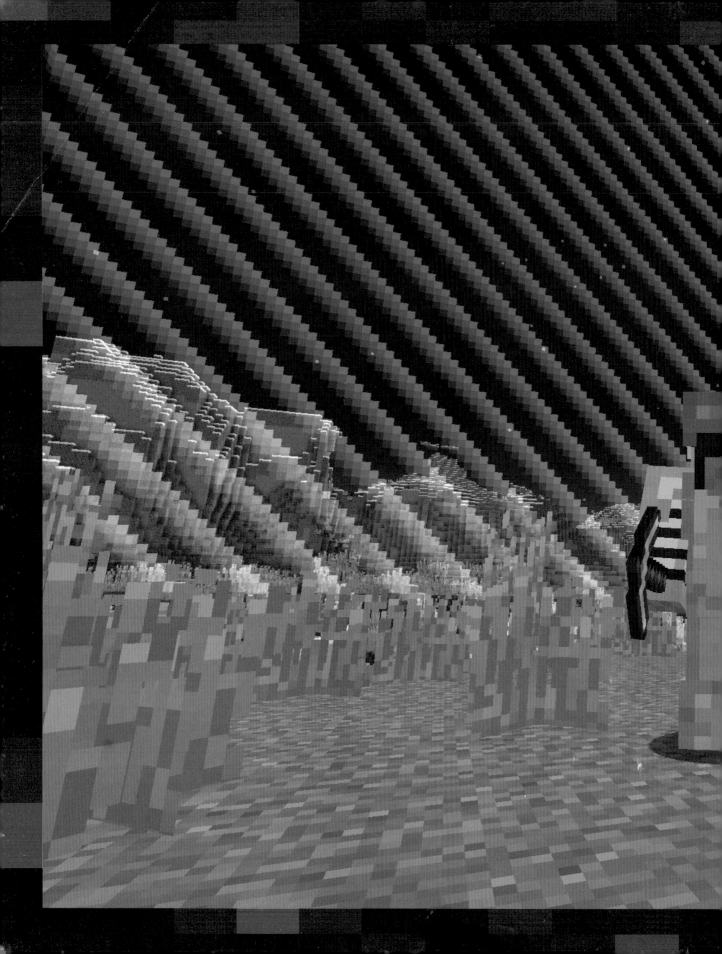

OCEAN MONUMENT, CONQUER AND REMODEL

SSP, Quest

Another rite of passage for the Minecraft adventurer is the conquering of an ocean monument. Although you can use it for a guardian/squid ink farm, there's a unique challenge in ridding the temple of its occupants, using sponges to

empty it of water, and making this magnificent structure your own.

ONE CHUNK BUILDS, TRY YOUR HAND AT

SSP, Building

If you're a builder, try making your edifices and homes take up just one chunk: 16x16 blocks. The challenge is the small space—for a greater challenge, add a sixteen-block limit to the height as well! These small builds also look fantastic in a 3D-rendered image using the Chunky app's isometric view. For more inspiration, see: Vidagarvia's "ChunkBuilds" at Imgur.com/a/HHlbY and Pixlriff's "One Chunk Build" videos on YouTube.

See also: Chunk, Chunky

ONE CHUNK CHALLENGE

SSP, Gameplay, Maps

In this challenge, you're not limited to building your base in a chunk—you have to stay in your solitary chunk forever (except for the Nether, visiting a stronghold if available, and the End.)

You can play this in your own world, using world borders or your own strength of will. You can also download One Chunk (or Single

Chunk) challenge maps. You can place or break blocks outside of your chunk as long as your feet are still chunk-bound.

The original one chunk challenge was Snocrash's original Hermit Chunk Challenge (which you can watch on YouTube). He plays

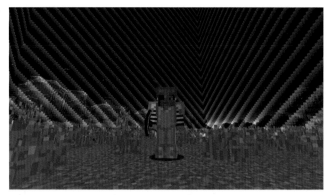

You could also define your chunk by enabling a world border that is sixteen blocks square.

In this map for Snocrash's Hermit Chunk Challenge, you'll have a tiny portion of swamp land to live on.

on a custom world with just two chunks in it: the chunk to live in and a chunk far away that holds part of a stronghold. You can download his challenge world from Snocrash.com. Another way to limit yourself to one vertical chunk is to add a world border. The world border itself isn't something you'll want to look at for long, so you can use fast graphics to not show it!

ORIGIN STORY, WRITE AN

OOG

Many of Minecraft's unusual mobs—like Endermen, ghasts, and creepers—seem to have their own mysterious stories. Why does a ghast have tears on its face? Why do Endermen get angry when you look at them? And do creepers just want to get close to you but can't handle it, exploding from all their pent-up . . . something? Are they made of leaves, like Notch, Minecraft's developer, suggested? What about ocean monuments, jungle temples, and the other abandoned structures you'll find in your world? Who built them, and why are they there? And then there's the Nether and the End—what is that all about? Dream up an explanation for one or more of Minecraft's mysteries, and write a story. If you like your story, share it on one of the several popular Minecraft forums.

Have you ever wondered what the inspiration was for a zombie pigman, or why it looks like it is also part skeleton?

P-Q

PACIFIST CHALLENGE

SSP, Gameplay

There are several variations of the Pacifist challenge: the main concept being no attacking *anyone*.

Rules are:

No weapons. No killing of any mobs, hostile or passive, by your own hand, for any reason. You can use traps, wolves, and golems, or you can run away. Armor, tools, and fishing and eating fish are fine. And you can eat already-cooked meat from villagers.

However, to survive hostile mobs, you'll need to avoid them entirely, run away, block yourself in until you can plan your escape, or set a trap that prevents them from reaching you.

In this challenge, you can use the help of golems to help ward off mobs.

PARKOUR, MASTER THE ART OF

SSP, Skill

There are tons of parkour maps to play and parkour mini-games online. If you want to practice to get your skills up, here are some moves to get you going:

- Fall a hundred blocks beside a wall or pillar, and break your fall by placing a ladder to stand on.
- Crouch when you land in the middle of a ladder.
- Jump from and land on ice and cactus.

- Jump on slime blocks or slime block contraptions that can propel you.
- Multiple three- and four-block jumps in a row.

Create your own parkour maps with ladders, falls, slime blocks, and a full variety of jumps. The maximum distance you can jump without sprinting is two blocks. The maximum distance you can jump sprinting is four blocks. A block placed one block up counts toward the total jump blocks, so a three-block jump to a higher block counts as a four-block jump. The maximum jump distance to lower blocks and ladders is increased slightly. The maximum length for diagonal block jumps depend on the angle and height.

Tip: Look up right before and while jumping. This betters your chances of making the move.

PET CHALLENGE

SSP, Quest

Tame and name all the tamable animals in the game: ocelot, wolf, llama, horse, and parrot. Get every type (coloring) of tamed ocelot: black with white feet, orange with spots, orange with stripes, and Siamese (white with black feet). Get every variety of llama (brown, cream, white, gray), and of Parrot (blue, cyan, gray, green, and red). Get every type of horse—and there are a lot! There are seven base colors for horses and five marking types: none, stockings and blaze, paint (large spots), sooty (small spots), and snowflake apaloosa (patchy stripes). To cover all of these possibilities, you'll need thirty-five horses. And finally, don't forget the three horse variants: donkey, mule, and skeleton horse.

If you want a competition, play with others to see how fast you can get all the pets.

The seven base colors for horses, from left to right: black, brown, chestnut, creamy, dark brown, gray, and white.

PIXEL ART, MAKE

SSP, Quest

If you have somehow managed to avoid seeing any Pixel art, it is blocky, flat art made in Minecraft using one block for each "pixel." It is easiest to recreate small icons and already pixelated art (like Minecraft items) by copying this art using Minecraft blocks. If you'd like to expand your abilities, learn how to take an unpixellated image and render this in Minecraft with Pixel art. A basic technique is to take a digital image and reduce its size in pixels to be the height or width limit of the final block height or width you want. For example, take a cartoon image of a cat or another character. Paste it into any paint program and change the size of it to be very small, say, sixty-four pixels high. This will make the image so small that the lines and filled in areas are now pixelated. Then, so that you can see it better, increase the size of the image by 200 or 400 percent, or larger if necessary. This should now be a pretty good guide for where to put what colors of pixels to replicate this art.

This image of a pear (top left) is made into pixel art by reducing its size to some fifty pixels high (top center), adding guidelines to view the pixels that will become blocks (top right), and then using this last image at left as a guide for selecting blocks and placing them in the Minecraft world.

PLAY, PUT ON A

SMP, Quest

Stage a play with your friends in Minecraft! Unlike an edited video, a play occurs in real time and on a single stage. How fancy you want to get with costumes (skins) and sets is up to you. Set up the stage and "chairs" for an audience, write your skits, and practice for the big event. Invite other players along to be the audience. You can type dialogue into Minecraft's chat box, or use headphones and microphones and communicate in a Discord voice channel. You'll want to be mindful of short attention spans, so keep your play short and sweet! If a friend can record video of the play, even better.

PRISON SERVER, PLAY ON A

SMP, Server

Prison is a very popular style of multiplayer-server gameplay. You start out as the lowest class of prisoner and must earn your way up to the higher levels. To earn your way, you must earn in-game currency or points by chopping wood or mining coal and other ores. As you progress, you can buy better tools and access better mines, sometimes a plot of building land or the ability to sell items. There are PvP-allowed areas to watch out for, depending on whether you want to PvP or not. It's a full-on grind to get to the top, although mining

At the bottom of the ladder in prison, you'll be mining at the lowest level of mine to get ores and sell them to finance better goods and loot.

is usually tweaked to go much faster than in Vanilla Minecraft. Like most other multiplayer public servers that feature a style of gameplay like Prison, Economy, and Factions, you're likely to be inundated with advertisements to buy perks for money. What this means is that players who spend more money can gain more powerful tools and perks. The Minecraft EULA (end-user license agreements) specifies that perks can't be sold to players to give them an advantage in the game, so if your server is abiding by the rules, there should be a free way for you to acquire the same types of perks given paying players.

See also: Faction Server, Economy Server

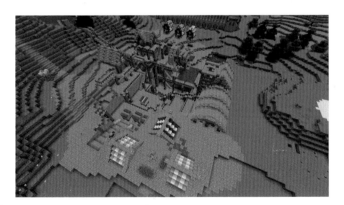

This detailed quarry with a treadwheel crane, storage area, water wheel, covered wagons, and tents for day laborers was created by reddit user /u/ oneaxetea.

QUARRY, BUILD A

SSP, Building

If you've enjoyed sprucing up your strip mines to look like real working mines, or even fantasy mines, try your hand at creating a quarry or open-pit mine. In real life, quarries are used to excavate stone, gravel, sand, and slate. Open-pit mines are used to excavate minerals. Quarries can be impressive structures—reaching deep into the ground, with lanes along the walls for construction vehicles to travel down to the bottom and back up, or supports to prevent cave-ins. There are ancient quarries and modern quarries and abandoned quarries filled partway with water. Look online for pictures of quarries and open-pit mines for a little inspiration.

QUIDDITCH, PLAY

SSP, Maps

If you are a Harry Potter fan, you're not alone. You can find many player-made maps online for playing Quidditch, exploring Hogwarts, or visiting the village of Hogsmeade!

See also: Maps, Creative Maps

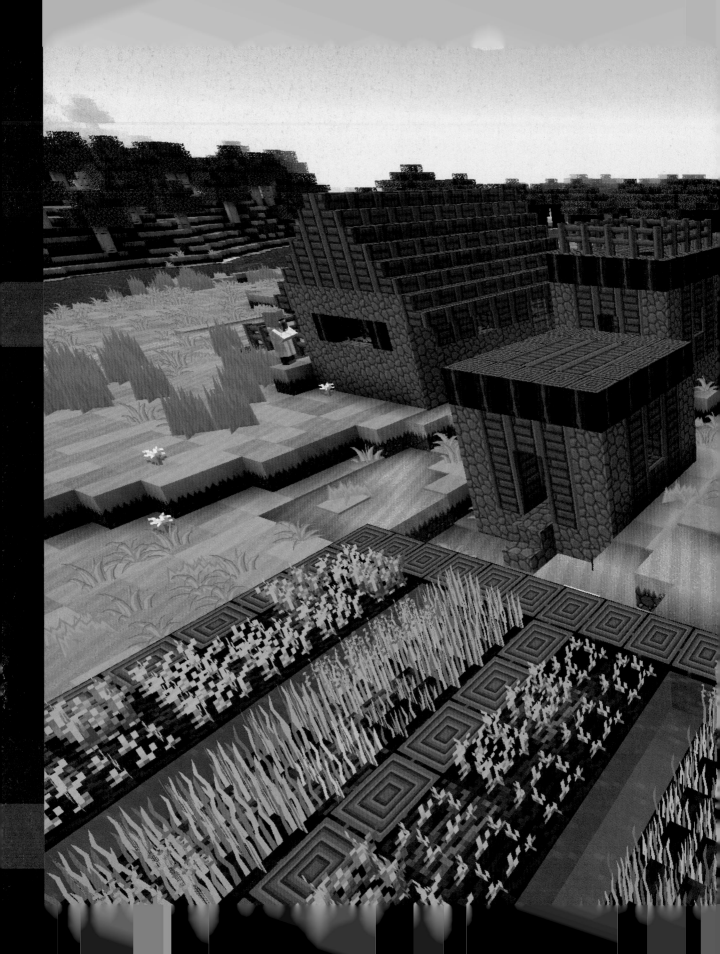

RECORD COLLECTOR, BE THE

SSP, Quest

There are twelve very rare music discs in Minecraft to collect and play in your jukebox. They can't be crafted. You'll find a few in dungeon chests, but you'll need to practice the art of getting a skeleton to kill a creeper. If you're unsuccessful getting both to follow you with the skeleton in the rear, trap them one in front of the other. If you stand in front of the creeper, the skeleton shooting at you should hit the creeper instead.

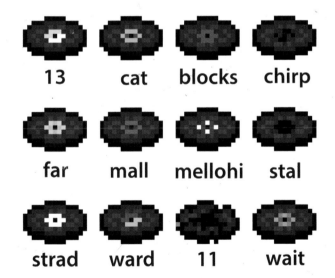

13   cat   blocks   chirp

far   mall   mellohi   stal

strad   ward   11   wait

The twelve music discs of Minecraft and what they are called.

REDSTONE CIRCUITS, LEARN

SSP, Skill

If you've dabbled with some redstone contraptions but you'd like to learn more and make your own creations, learn the basic redstone circuits. These are basically logic gates and arrangements of redstone and other components for transmitting redstone power in different ways. For example, there are several ways to transmit a redstone signal upward; these are vertical transmission circuits. Pulse circuits control the length in time of a pulse, or change single pulses into multiple pulses, etc. Clock circuits are designed to continually output a pulse at regular intervals. In addition, logic gates are designed to allow or prevent redstone power transmission depending on the combination of input power signals. A NOT gate inverts a signal. If the input signal is off, then the output signal is on, and vice versa.

Understanding how these components work and how they can work together will help you tremendously in inventing your own contraptions. You can learn about them on the Minecraft official wiki at Minecraft.gamepedia.com, and you can also find books about redstone contraptions and circuits in your library and in stores.

This NOT gate (a type of logic gate) inverts a signal. If the original signal is off, then the output is on, and vice versa.

This OR gate (another type of logic gate) takes many inputs, and if any are on, the output signal is on.

This is a vertical transmission circuit that allows you to send a signal upward.

HISTORICAL OR MYTHOLOGICAL BUILDING, RECREATE A

SSP, Building

While reconstructing the Louvre may be out of the running for most of us humble builders, there are thousands of famous buildings that can be recreated by a single person or group of friends with limited time. There's the Eiffel Tower, Noah's Ark, Great Pyramid of Giza, the Acropolis, and fairy tale buildings like Rapunzel's Tower. You may have an historical building nearby you that you can recreate. For more inspiration, search online for more famous buildings from history, mythology, and religion.

RESOURCE PACK, PLAY WITH A

SSP, Gameplay

You can really change how your world looks and feels by playing with a resource pack (sometimes called a texture pack). A resource pack can change how objects and items look; it can also change sounds, models, music, fonts, and the opening splash text. Resource packs are designed for a particular version of Minecraft, so if you

The SapixCraft512 resource pack uses different models and textures for wheat, grass, logs, cobble, planks, and more.

find one you want to try out, you need to make sure there is a version of it for your game version.

You can preview and download resource packs at several websites, like Resourcepack. net and Curseforge.net. After you download a resource pack, place the zipped folder into the resource packs folder in your Minecraft game files folder. Open Minecraft again, and click Options, the Resource Packs. In the Resource Packs window, the packs the game recognizes (outside of the default game resource pack) are listed in the left window. Select a resource pack and click the arrow to move it to the active resource pack window.

ROLE PLAY

SSP, Gameplay

Lots of games include role-playing as part of the game. Role-playing means you play as a type of character, and you're often limited to the types of activities and skills this character would have. While you can play with RPG mods in Minecraft, you can set up your own role to play by in sandbox Vanilla Minecraft. Make up a character or choose a popular type of character, and figure out what the character would and wouldn't do, and what their goals would be. Lots of challenges are inspired by the idea of playing a character, like the Hermit Challenge and the Pacifist Challenge. But your character can be anything you dream up, from a Lapis-obsessed elf to a zombie-fighting warrior.

SANCTUARY, BUILD A MOB

SSP, Building

Build a sanctuary for a mob of your choice that you feel needs a safe place to call their own without being eaten or killed. This could be farm animals, parrots, the misunderstood spider, spitting llamas, or the much-maligned green-coated villagers. (If you choose a hostile or neutral mob, name them so they don't despawn!) Plan out a space with elements you think they'd really like, whether it's grass to eat, walls to climb, or doors to open and shut constantly.

A zombie's perfect sanctuary might include protection from the sun and plenty of tasty villagers!

SCAVENGER HUNT

SSP, SMP, Competition

There are a number of ways to set up a scavenger hunt in Minecraft. First, you can set up a list of items or blocks you must find in the Minecraft world. The winner is the player who returns first with all the items. Second, you can set a time limit—thirty real-life minutes or an hour—to find as many different Minecraft items as possible. Each item is worth a point, and the winner is the player with the most points at the end of the time limit. If you want to get really fancy, you could set up a scavenger hunt for friends on a multiplayer server, with riddles to be solved in order to find new items. There are lots of scavenger hunt guides online with tips on planning hunts and riddles to use.

Example hunts:

- Items beginning with the letter M
- A Minecraft alphabet requiring one item for each letter of the alphabet (e.g., andesite, blue orchid, cobblestone, etc.)

See also: Bingo, Get Everything, Iron Man

SHIP, BUILD A

SSP, Building

Building a ship is one of the hardest building challenges in Minecraft. It's harder than building a sphere, for which you can easily find a template.

The difficulty lies in making all of the slightly different curves for the shape of the hull, the bow, the deck, the stern, and any sails and rigging. If you are up for the challenge, first decide what type of ship you're interested in making: a yacht, eighteenth-century warship, aircraft carrier, battleship, Viking longship, clipper, etc. Find photographs and drawings of this type of ship online and any images of this ship type built in Minecraft. To get the proportions right, try to find details and dimensions of the lengths, widths, and heights of the ship, ship elements, and sails, along with positioning, from real life versions. Convert these as closely as possible into blocks (1 block is 1 meter). You can use these measurements to set out a rough outline in Minecraft of where these parts will be in your own boat.

The first step is to build the keel—the bottom spine of the ship. You will want to include the curves in the keel. Once the keel is finished, build out the hull—the outer body. There are several curves to keep in mind. There are curves that go from keel to deck. There are also curves that run between the bow and stern. In addition, the deck itself may be raised at the bow and the stern. Once you've finished the keel, hull, and deck, you can position the other elements, masts, bowsprit, guns, forecastle, etc. The sails will be the hardest part of the build, and for these you may want to refer to how these are handled by other Minecraft builders. In general, with the most effective sails, blocks of wool are placed to look as if wind is blowing out the central area of each sail.

Because ship building is so difficult, you can find tutorials online to read how other Minecraft builders approach this challenge.

SKIN, MAKE YOUR OWN CUSTOM

OOG, Software

If you are tired of wearing a Skin made by someone else, and especially if you are still sporting an Alex or Steve Skin, then it's time to craft your own unique look. The easiest way to make

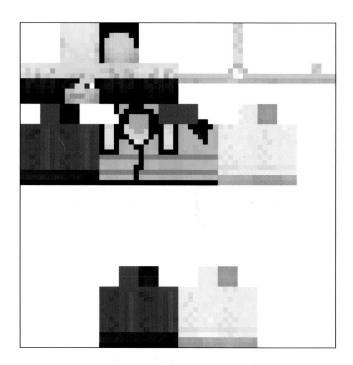

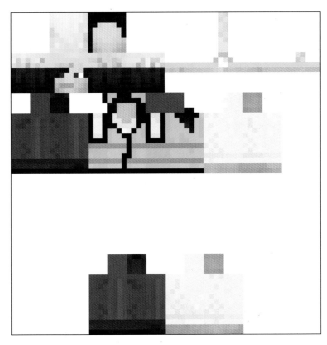

A Skin file is an image file only sixty-four pixels square (see top image). The bottom image is the same file zoomed up, so you can see the differently colored pixels.

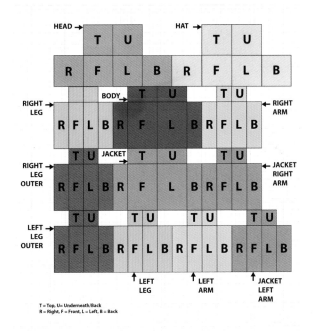

This template shows what part of a Skin image file is used for what part of a player's body.

your own Skin is to start with someone else's and then change colors and modify it using an online tool like the one at Needcoolshoes.com. Here you can search for Skins or Skin parts (like hats, boots, etc.). When you're finished, you can upload it directly to Minecraft.net to change your Skin or save it to your computer first.

SKY HIGH, LIVE

SSP, Gameplay

Instead of living underwater or on an island, move to the sky. Build yourself a massive floating geodesic dome or an archipelago of sky islands and live above the clouds. If you want animals there with you or villagers, you'll need to figure out a way to get them there!

You can also make this into a SkyBlock challenge by giving yourself a limited amount of time to build your air base and limited resources to start with.

See also: SkyBlock

SKYBLOCK, PLAY MODDED

SSP, Modded

In the world of modpacks, there is a popular category called SkyBlock. Unlike Vanilla

SkyBlock, you don't start out with any water or any lava. You will often start out on just a few blocks of dirt and grass, with one or two saplings to get started. You'll have to use Sky-Block-designed mods to gather water from rain, and liquify cobblestone to create lava. A modded SkyBlock may use mods that enable you to get ore from hammering down gravel, sand, and cobblestone and sieving the products; or it may have other ways of allowing you to get these resources. SkyBlock modpacks often come with quest books, and can be a great way to start learning about mods.

SKYBLOCK, PLAY VANILLA

SSP, Map

SkyBlock, sometimes called Sky Island, is another classic survival challenge, inspired by the Survival Island challenge. The difference here is that your island is up in the air, floating in the void, and very small! The original Sky-Block map by Noobcrew was created in Minecraft 1.4.7, but it still works. (You can also find other Vanilla SkyBlock island maps if you prefer). In the original SkyBlock challenge, you spawn on a little island in the sky with one tree and one chest holding one bucket of lava and one ice block in it. A couple dozen blocks away

is a floating cuboid of sand that has a cactus growing on it and one block of sand, and a cactus floats in the air some blocks away, unreachable until you can bridge over. You can download the map on Minecraftmaps.com. The creator has posted various sets of challenges to complete with the map, both at Minecraftmaps. com and Minecraftforum.net. Some skills you will need to survive on SkyBlock include: making a cobble generator, making an infinite water source, lighting a portal without flint and steel, using water as a ladder to build below the block you are standing on, how to stop water turning into ice, and how to avoid making floating sand blocks drop into the void below.

In this original SkyBlock map by Noobcrew, you'll have a tiny island with some resources.

SPEEDRUN, DO A

SSP, Competition

In a speedrun, a gamer tries to complete a game or in-game task as fast as possible. The game is video-recorded and timed for accuracy.

In Minecraft, the game ends after the dragon is killed when the player returns to the Overworld through the End portal. Visit Speedrun.com/mc to view the leaderboards for the different categories of Minecraft speedruns. You can also find videos from the players' speedruns, as well as guides and instructions for entering the fray. Before attempting a speedrun yourself, learn the tricks and tactics already found by previous speedrunners by watching their entry videos. In many of these videos, however, there's little talking to explain what the gamer is doing. However, some well-known

YouTubers have participated in the Any% set seed glitchless run, including AntVenom (fourteenth place) and SethBling (thirtieth place), and their videos are well worth watching.

Some speedrun terms to be aware of: *Any%* means a speedrun for completing the game. *Set seed* means using the same seed for all speedrun entries. *Random seed* means letting the game determine the seed on each run. *Glitchless* means not using any bugs or glitches in the game to help speed up your run. *TAS* means tool-assisted speedrun (for example, a tool might be using controller inputs to quickly press multiple buttons, faster than a player would normally be able to).

Currently, players are completing Minecraft end speedruns (Any% set seed glitchless category) in under eight minutes. Player Thee-Sizzler from Canada is currently in first place as of writing this book, with an Any% Glitchless Set Seed run of seven minutes, eleven seconds, and 860 milliseconds. That's basically seven minutes from spawning in the world to finishing the dragon fight and stepping into the End portal. The fastest Any% TAS (thus far) was made by Geosquare in ninety-five seconds! (See this on YouTube on Geosquare's channel.) Set your timer to zero and stretch your fingers!

STRONGHOLDS, FIND, EXPLORE, AND EXCAVATE

SSP, Quest

Strongholds are mysterious labyrinths of corridors, sprinkled with special types of rooms, like cells, libraries, and well rooms. Like many other Minecraft structures, they're procedurally generated. An algorithm generates them in a similar way as the Minecraft landscape is generated, so each stronghold is unique. Some may be smaller than others, broken up by ravines, and others may be more fully formed. Find all the types of unique rooms that can be generated in a Stronghold: spiral staircases, End portal rooms; bridge rooms, libraries, stone pillar rooms, fountain rooms, storerooms (two-story rooms with a ladder in between), prison cells, and chest corridors.

In Java Edition, there are rings of strongholds, up to a total of 128 strongholds, as per the official Minecraft wiki. The rings are centered on 0,0. How many can you find?

Ring 1: three strongholds, radius: 1408 to 2688 blocks

Ring 2: six strongholds, radius 4480 to 5760 blocks

Ring 3: ten strongholds, radius 7552 to 8832 blocks

Ring 4: fifteen strongholds, radius 10624 to 11904 blocks

Ring 5: twenty-one strongholds, radius 13696 to 14976 blocks

Ring 6: twenty-eight strongholds, radius 16768 to 18048 blocks

Ring 7: thirty-six strongholds, radius 19840 to 21120 blocks

Excavating a stronghold can show you the scale of the structure from an outside view.

Ring 8: nine strongholds, radius 22912 to 24192 blocks

Finally, if you are a fan of digging stuff, excavate an entire stronghold. If you've found a few, pick one that seems most well-formed and not broken up by mineshafts and ravines. Dig out all the dirt, stone, and caves around it so you can view it in its entirety.

STRUCTURE, FIND EVERY GENERATED BUILDING

SSP, Quest

Find one of every type of generated building structure in Minecraft. Currently, this list includes abandoned mineshaft, desert temple, desert village, desert well, dungeon, End city, End ship, igloo, jungle temple, Nether fortress, ocean monument, plains village, savanna village, shipwreck, stronghold, taiga village, underwater ruins, witch hut, and woodland mansion.

You can make this a race by limiting the time you can spend finding structures or by measuring the amount of time needed to find every structure.

SUPERFLAT WORLD, LIVE IN A

SSP, Gameplay

Make your new world a Superflat world. When you create a new world, choose Superflat for the world type and don't customize it. There'll be no mining for you, but there will be villages, the Nether, and lots and lots of slimes to battle. If you want a specific challenge or quests to add in to your experience, visit Minecraftforum.net and search for Superflat challenge to find a variety of takes on this gameplay challenge.

Jungle temples are relatively hard to find, because the Jungle biome itself is fairly rare.

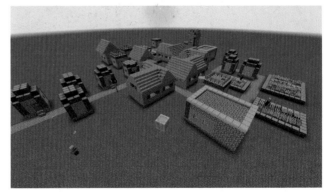

It's easy to find villages and slimes in a Superflat world.

For an even harder Superflat challenge, go flatcore. Create your Superflat world, but make the game mode hardcore! If you want to find tips for playing this way, search for "flatcore." **See also:** Swampcore

SURVIVAL ISLAND

SSP, Gameplay

This challenge is a classic Minecraft mission: Can you survive on a small remote island, far from the mainland? This challenge began as a survival map posted on Minecraftforum. net, but the idea became so popular that it has become a genre of gameplay, with many variations, maps, and seeds to use. It also spawned similar challenges, like the SkyBlock challenge. However, the basic premise is the same in all survival island challenges: you cannot leave the island! You can mine but must come back up to your island.

One Java Edition 1.12.2 seed for a survival island is -3057195824021022322.

For a full challenge, add the goal to reach the End and defeat the Ender Dragon. The only time you can leave the island is to find your stronghold. Once found, you can only travel to and from it by using Nether portals.

The original Survival Island map by Ashien is no longer available, but you can find dozens of seeds and other survival island maps online and posted on Minecraft forums. If you aren't using a map, you'll want to find a seed that is compatible with the version of Minecraft you are using. You can also use a map explorer like Amidst to find a seed.

SWAMPCORE, TEST YOUR SURVIVAL SKILLS IN

SSP, Gameplay

If hardcore isn't quite hard enough for you, you may be ready for Swampcore. It's hardcore with an unforgiving twist: you must survive on a world that is Superflat and Swampland biome only—during a permanent thunderstorm.

You can find Swampcore maps online or you can create your own hardcore, swamp-only world. For Minecraft 12.2, you can use a preset setting from a preset generator online, or the following:

Swampcore is Superflat, swamp-only, permanent thunderstorm, hardcore survival. I'm not sure it could get any harder!

3;9*minecraft:bedrock, minecraft:dirt,minecraft:grass;6; biome_1,decoration,lake,lava_lake

If you make your own Swampcore world with Minecraft's world settings, turn cheats on, so you can enter the command for (almost) permanent thunder. Alternately, create the world without cheats and then temporarily open your world to LAN, allow cheats on, and then type the command to change the weather to a thunderstorm:

/weather thunder 1000000

You'll be able to find a tiny bit of stone and ore around lava lakes, aboveground fossils, witch huts, plenty of slime, and monsters galore.

See also: Flatcore, Superflat World, Hardcore

TERRAFIRMACRAFT, PLAY

SSP, Modded

If you've ever thought Minecraft makes chopping down trees and making furnaces a bit too easy, then the mod TerraFirmaCraft may be for you. This mod, created by Bioxx, reworks Minecraft survival to be a bit more authentic and a lot more difficult. Its motto is "Survival Mode as It Should Have Been." With it, you progress through three stages: the stone age, then a casting age (pottery, copper, and bronze), and finally on to the iron age and its smithing system. This mod is deep and detailed and changes much of Minecraft survival, so you'll need the aid of the wiki (wiki.terrafirmacraft. com). It also helps to follow along with one of Let's Play videos you'll find on YouTube. You can play this mod by itself. However, it has also inspired multiple other add-on mods to further expand on the premise of a more authentic survival, and you can find these collected in various TerraFirmaCraft modpacks. Get ready to bang some stones together!

There are a score of new types of stone and ore in TerraFirmaCraft, along with the ability to have mining cave-ins.

TIME TRAVEL THROUGH MINECRAFT

SSP, Quest

Minecraft was released in very early versions for the gaming community to test, respond to, and play. The game has gone through various stages of evolution since Minecraft's developer, Markus "Notch" Persson, first developed it (the pre-classic stage), released the first testing versions, and finally began released official versions. Early versions don't have the crafting system or all the mobs we know and love, and they are often buggy. But with the magic of computers, we can still play the early versions of the PC Java game. You specify what version of Minecraft you want to play in the official Minecraft launcher. With the very early versions, use at your own risk and be prepared for bugs. Create a different world for each version that you check out! You can read more about the history of the development of Minecraft on the official wiki, Minecraft.gamepedia.com/Version_history.

In the pre-release, development stage called Early Classic Creative, developers were working on generating terrain and different types of blocks. This version, 0.0.11a, features a wild Steve spawning and jumping around the world!

TNT OLYMPICS, PLAY SETHBLING'S

SMP, Competition

In 2012, redstone engineer extraordinaire and popular YouTuber SethBling released his minigame map, SethBling's Minecraft TNT Olympics. Set in an amazing stadium, the map set up a ten-event decathlon that includes the javelin throw, balance beam, and synchronized swimming. Each event involves TNT explosions in some way! Download the map from Planetminecraft.com and compete with your friends. Watch the original athletes for the first Official TNT Olympics face off on their YouTube miniseries: SethBling, Etho (EthosLab), Captain-Sparklez, and AntVenom.

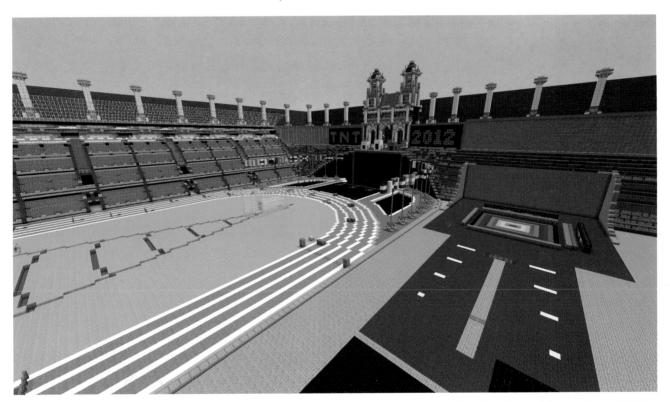

SethBling's famous TNT Olympics map is designed for Olympic-style games that involve a fair number of TNT explosions.

TREASURE HUNT, SUNKEN

SMP, Competition

Find and claim as many sunken pirate ships as you can in thirty minutes! Mark each find with a sign to stop other players from claiming the point. Each pirate ship counts as one point and whoever has the most points wins.

Variation: Add two additional points for each buried treasure found.

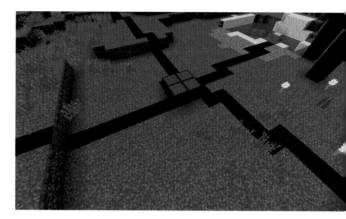

In this challenge, you can't go anywhere without being on a log connected to your spirit tree.

Chop it down except for the bottom block. The bottom block is your tree heart. From here, you can only travel on logs harvested from your spirit tree, or from the saplings generated by your spirit tree. You'll be building out the roots of your spirit tree to reach everywhere you go in your world: mining, farming, hunting. You can only jump off briefly to gather items dropped on the ground itself. For full rules, visit Minecraftforum.net and search for Challenge—The Tree Spirit.

In a variation of this competition, assign points to the types of treasure you can find from ships, and whoever collects the most booty wins.

TREE SPIRIT CHALLENGE

SSP, Gameplay

Originally created by Cthulhu725 and formalized by players on Minecraftforum.net like Lilariel, the Tree Spirit challenge is similar to the Dwarven Heartstone Challenge. Start a new world and pick a tree to be your spirit tree.

TWITCH LAUNCHER, INSTALL MODPACKS WITH THE

OOG, software

The Twitch launcher is the easiest way to install mods and modpacks. You can install the launcher from App.twitch.tv/download.

What can be confusing about the launcher is that it is combined with the Twitch streaming app, a general games launcher, and mod installation for other games. To get to the right location for Minecraft mods, click Mods and then Minecraft. Here is where you can browse modpacks from the official Twitch/Curse/FTB (Feed the Beast) team or other modpack creators. Select a modpack and click Install. Once installed, click play. You can even create a custom profile and add mods one at a time for your own modpack.

See also: MultiMC

TWO BY TWO

Advancement

To get this in-game Husbandry advancement, you'll need to breed each of these ten animals: chicken (breed with wheat seeds, melon seeds, pumpkin seeds, or beetroot seeds), cow (wheat), horse (golden apple, golden carrot), llama (hay bale), mooshroom (wheat), ocelot, pig (beetroot, carrot, potato), rabbit (dandelion, carrot, golden carrot), sheep (wheat), and wolf (any raw or cooked meat or zombie flesh).

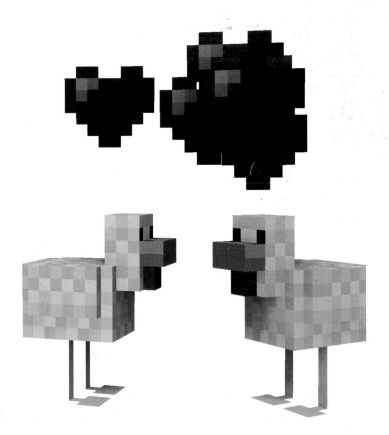

UGLY BLOCK, MAKE OVER AN

SSP, Building

Choose the ugliest block, to you, in Minecraft, and use it in a build in a way that makes it look good. If you like all the blocks, choose one your friends don't like, so you can show them how it's done. Some top ugly block contenders may be purpur, diorite, and granite, but you may have your own least favorite!

UHC, PLAY A GAME OF

SMP, mini-game

The Ultra Hardcore Game, or UHC, is a long-form multiplayer game that can take many in-game days and up to several hours. It was invented by Minecraft YouTuber Ethos (EthosLab) on the private Mindcrack server that many popular YouTubers have played on. In UHC,

Golden apples are a valuable resource in a UHC, so it's wise to spend time cutting down oak trees. The oak trees in a swamp have more leaf blocks than others, so a swamp is a great starting place.

players or teams are spawned in different areas of a new world and must battle to be last man or team standing. The game is played in ultra hardcore mode. UHC games may be played with additional restrictions, too, depending on the server or agreement by players. For example, there may be a shrinking world border, or a time limit, or a restriction against using certain potions or going to the Nether. There may be a rule prohibiting PvP for the first half hour or so. During the first part of the game, players spend a fair amount of time gathering resources until they're geared up and ready to start battling others. Many public mini-game servers host their own versions of UHC, including speed UHC versions that only take ten minutes or so.

ULTRA HARDCORE MODE, PLAY IN

SSP, SMP, gameplay

Ultra hardcore is a user-invented game mode as well as a multiplayer game usually called UHC. If hardcore doesn't sound hard enough, ultra hardcore mode will get your teeth a-chattering. In ultra hardcore, if you get smacked by a zombie, your health points go down and they will stay down. You can't eat to get better. The only thing you can do to heal is craft and use a healing or regeneration potion, a golden apple, and beacons with resistance and regeneration effects.

To create an ultra hardcore world, you'll need to use the command /gamerule naturalRegeneration false. To use commands, you'll need to create the world with cheats on and then be very diligent and honorable and not use any other cheats. To make cheating less tempting, use a temporary LAN version of your world to execute the regeneration command. To do this, open your new hardcore world and click Escape. Then click Open to LAN. (This just allows your world to be shared on your local network, if you have one. But you don't need a network for this trick to work.) Now you can change some world settings. Turn on Allow Cheats. Click

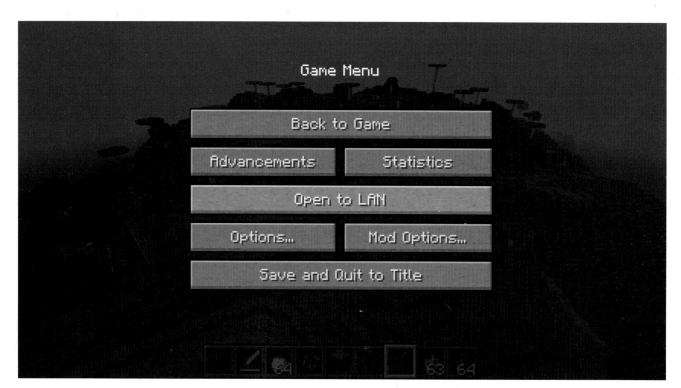

To make a temporary LAN version of your world, click Open to LAN on your Game Menu screen and then turn cheats on so you can execute a command.

Start LAN world. Enter the command into the chat box, press Enter, and make sure you see the game response, "Game rule naturalRegeneration has been updated to false." If you see an error message, then try again. Finally, click Escape again and then Save and Quit to Title. Now you can reopen your world as a regular single-player world that has no natural regeneration. Craft a shield as quickly as possible!

UNDERWATER LIVING

SSP, Gameplay

Build your underwater home, or at least the start of it. Then leave the sunlit surface with an inventory of supplies to live only below the waves. You can't return to terra firma—ever. You can mine, as long as you're in the Ocean Biomes. But how long will you last before you go crazy? In the standard community challenge format, you've got one day on hard difficulty to gather materials. Then you must head

underwater to build a permanent base. Again, no leaving for the surface!

UNDERWATER HOME, BUILD AN

SSP, Building

Building your first underwater home is a rite-of-passage challenge. Tools and techniques that you can use to help this endeavor include Potion of Water Breathing, Potion of Night Vision, Aqua Affinity helmet, Depth Strider boots, Respiration helmet, "excavating" the volume of water you are building in by dropping sand or gravel to replace water blocks, conduits, and sponges.

A good place to start your underwater home could be an underwater ruin.

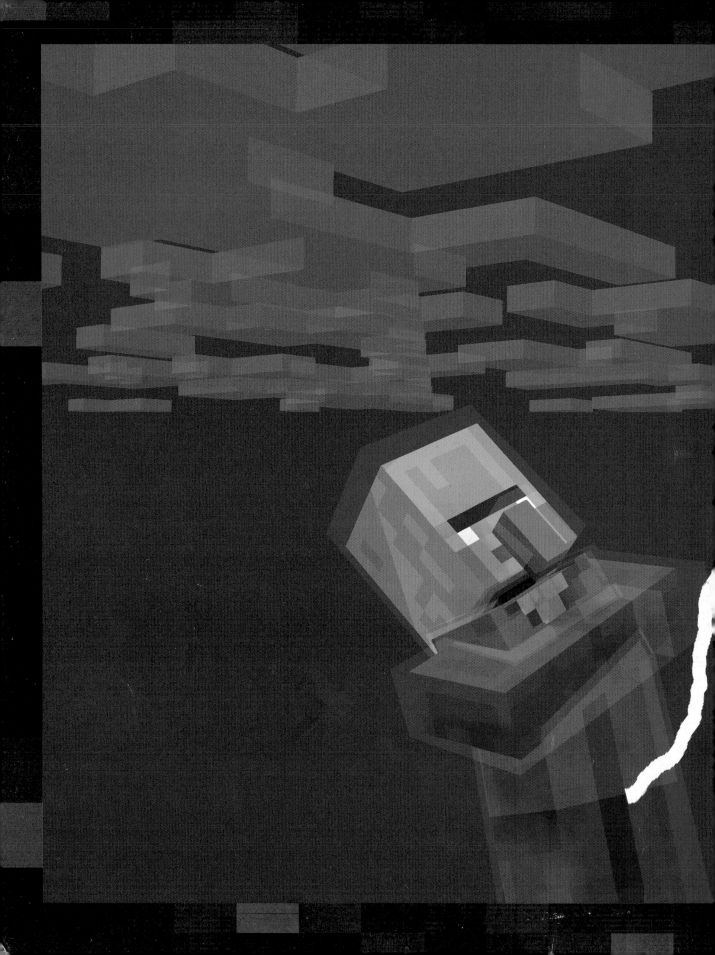

VAMPIRE, LIVE AS A

SSP, SMP, Gameplay, Modded

In Minecraft, the player is always Steve or Alex or your own variation: a "human" playing in a world of monsters. How would you like to try playing *as* the monster? You can role-play as a vampire with challenge restrictions like coming out only at night, living on zombie flesh and raw meat, and murdering villagers.

For even more immersion in vampire gameplay, there's an amazing mod: the Vampirism Mod. With this mod, you'll have to sleep at night in a coffin, terrorize villagers, drink blood (Bleh! Bleh!), and defeat vampire hunters. Your first challenge will be to be bitten by a vampire or acquire some vampire blood you can use to inflict the *Sanguinare Vampiris* condition that will change you slowly to undead. (Of course, if role-playing as a monster doesn't appeal, the mod does allow you to play as a vampire hunter.)

In Java Vampire's role-playing YouTube series, "Vampirism—A Vampire's Journey," he creates a creepy, old mansion atop a hill and terrorizes the nearby villages.

VEGAN CHALLENGE

SSP, Gameplay

This challenge has only a few simple rules: no eating animals or using animal products (like milk, leather, or eggs) and no killing animals. However, included in "animals" is all passive and neutral mobs. The only mobs you can

attack are hostile mobs that are attacking you: no automated farming of mobs allowed!

There's a lot on the okay-to-eat list: apples, beetroot, beetroot soup, bread, carrots (regular and golden), cookies, dried kelp, potatoes, carrots, beet soup, melon, and mushroom stew. When you are rolling in gold, add in golden apples and golden carrots! Of all the vegan options, the food with the most food points and saturation are golden carrot, beetroot soup, and mushroom stew. After this, bread and baked potatoes are a good choice. No killing cows for leather, so no leather armor, and you'll need to find a solution if you want to enchant. You'll need to find string to use for wool, or find an already crafted bed to sleep in. Get extra points

for not killing the End Dragon but making it to an End city regardless!

If this is too much, try a more forgiving vegetarian challenge (milk, eggs, and other animal products allowed), or a pescatarian challenge (same as the Vegetarian, but with fish!).

VERY VERY FRIGHTENING

Advancement

To complete this in-game advancement, you'll need to use a trident enchanted with channeling during a storm to throw lightning at a villager. And you remember what happens when villagers are struck by lightning, right?

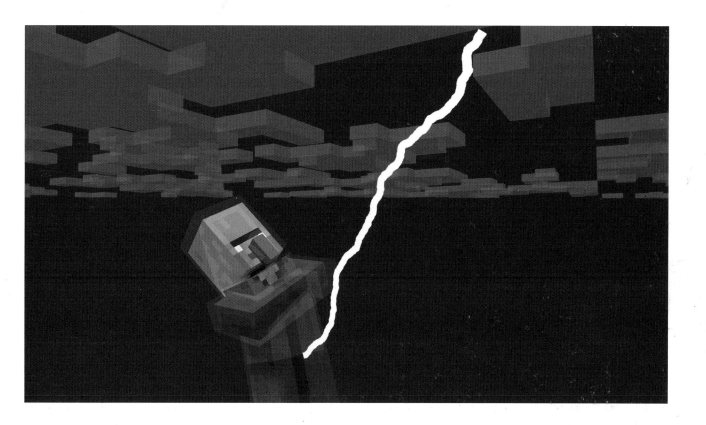

VILLAGE, REMODEL A

SSP, Building

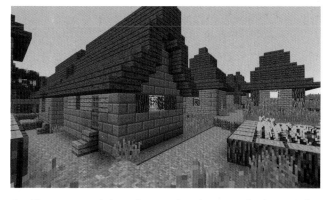

A village remodel can be as simple as replacing roofs and the cobblestone.

Whether you are fond or not of Minecraft's village architecture, the villages really do look pretty much the same. And that makes them a great opportunity to try your own hand at village architecture. You can add touches and customizations to the existing buildings, or you can replace buildings in their entirety. It might be nice to see some villagers living in an igloo settlement or a medieval town for a change. Remodeling villages is a classic activity in Minecraft, and you'll see many players show their remodels on forums and YouTube.

VILLAGES, SAVE YOUR

SSP, Quest

Put on your superhero cape and save your villagers! You'll need to light up the villages properly, fence, or wall them in. Close up any dangerous drops to ravines or cave entrances nearby, and remove cacti, lava pools, and other hazards. Get villagers up and out of water and close off access for falling in the water. If the village is too small to generate its own iron golem (ten villagers and twenty-one doors), create one for them. Prevent zombie sieges in larger villages (twenty-plus villagers and ten-plus doors) by staying outside of the village from midnight till dawn.

Even more heroic: save a zombie village and its inhabitants. Two percent of villages are zombie villages, populated with zombie villagers and missing doors and torches. You'll want splash potions of weakness to throw at the villagers and golden apples to heal them. When your villagers are restored to normal, continue on with the village safeguards.

One of the first steps in saving a village is preventing zombies coming in, with walls and lighting.

VILLAGE GROWTH CHALLENGE

SSP/SMP, Quest, Competition

How large can you expand a village, without resorting to just placing random doors everywhere? In this challenge, take a village and make it bigger. And then a little bigger. And then some more, until you have plenty of golems lumbering around. How many golems can you get?

You can only build real "homes" for the villagers—apartment buildings are acceptable. To be "real," a home or apartment building can have more than one door, but it must have at least one window for each door and at least two blocks between each door. Your village needs to look like a real village. Use the existing buildings as examples. You can substitute stores and other buildings for homes if you like—the villagers won't care—and it can add to your village's ambiance.

Now, the villagers will need farmers to hand out crops to them that they are willing to breed. You aren't allowed to throw bread or crops at the villagers yourself, or trade with them in order to help them breed. You're only allowed to build and prevent the villagers from hurting themselves or being hurt by zombies.

If you'd like a goal: How long does it take you to get to five iron golems spawning naturally? If you can compete with friends, with teams or players working on separate villages, what village is the first to spawn five golems? Adjust the challenge as you need! And if you love playing with villages, there are other village-related challenges out there. Google "Minecraft village challenge."

VILLAGER, LIVE AS A

SSP, Gameplay

Play through your game only as a villager. You are limited to living within villages and using items within the village limits or that you can trade for with villagers. You can mine beneath the village and increase the size of the village to increase villager count and trade possibilities. To travel, you'll need to find neighboring villages to sleep in and connect villages with railways.

You can find villager Skins to wear on your Steve or Alex model online, just to make it all more believable.

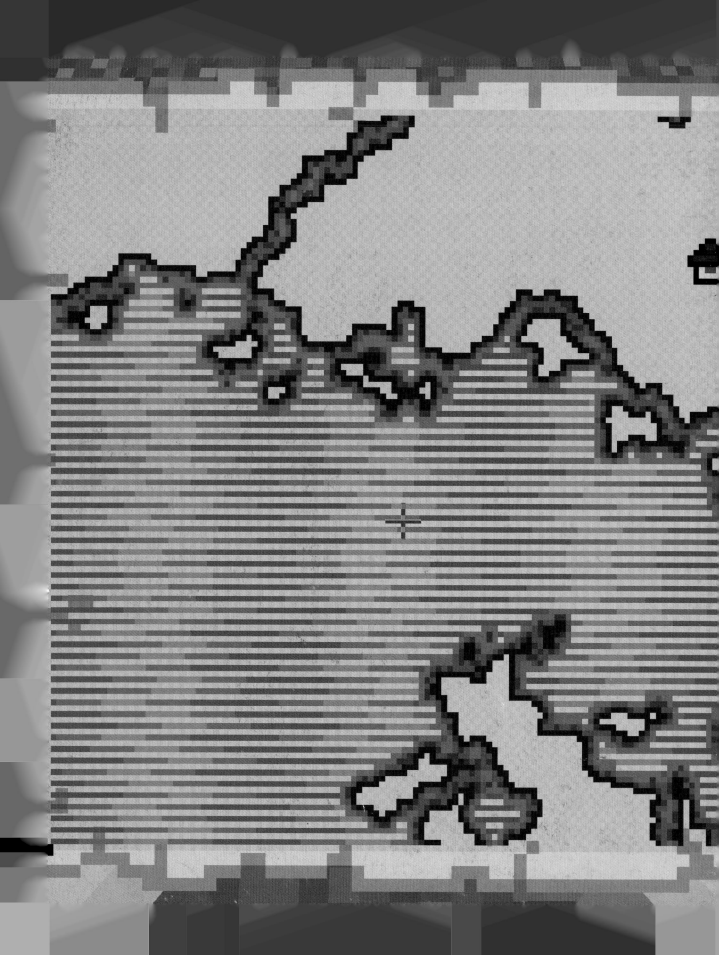

WATER WORLD

SSP, Gameplay

In this challenge, you can only build in deep ocean. Gather resources to start off with, including a lily pad. Use a boat to travel to deep ocean, where you can build your water-living kingdom. Pick a location where you can only see water from horizon to horizon. Use the lily pad to help place your first blocks above the water. You can travel to shore to gather farming resources, like seeds and sapling and animals, but everything must come back to your home above the waves. Will your water world be a series of linked fishing boats and rafts? A floating island paradise? A post-apocalyptic mishmash of industry and farms?

To make this challenge harder to cheat on, use Minecraft's World Type options to create a custom world that is mostly ocean!

WITHERING HEIGHTS

Advancement

To get this advancement, you need only be in the same 100-meter cube as a spawned Wither. If you are interested in having as little interaction with the Wither as possible, you have a few options. Conceivably, you could have a friend do this and have them be responsible for killing

the Wither, then leave the area ASAP. Or travel to a far, far location, one which you are happy to never return to, and plan your escape route (Elytra? Boat on ice? A fast horse?) Once you've chosen your location and set up your speedy exit, spawn the Wither and then race away. Once you're out of chunk loading range, (in single-player worlds, beyond your view distance) the Wither will remain frozen with that chunk unless you return.

WOODLAND MANSION, FIND AND EXPLORE A

SSP, Quest

At least once in your Minecraft career, take the time to find and explore a Woodlands Mansion. They're enormous, procedurally generated

buildings secluded in roofed forests. "Procedurally generated" means that the game spawns each one with an algorithm to locate different types of corridors, rooms, and staircases. Each mansion will be a little different. If you haven't seen one before, they can include map rooms, dining rooms, chest rooms, statue rooms, hidden staircases and treasure chests. They also include a few dangerous villagers: the Vindicator and the Evoker. However, if you have enchanted armor and weapons, you should be fine! (Make sure to set your spawn somewhere safe and nearby, in case you do die!)

They're typically very far from spawn, often easily 10,000 blocks, and you'll need an Explorer map from a Cartographer Villager to find one. It will be a long trek to get there, so an Elytra will be an enormous asset. If you don't have an Elytra, you could try using the Nether to travel longer distances faster.

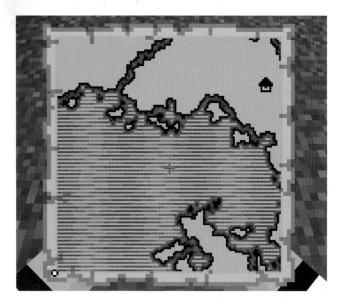
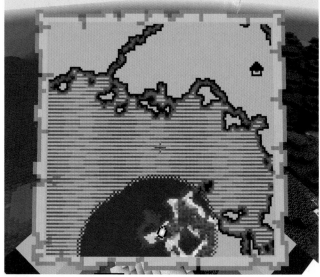

To find a woodland map, you'll need to buy one (left) from a cartographer. The white dot shows your position, usually far from the mansion. As you get closer (right), the white dot will move closer to the mansion icon and the map will also fill out with color.

You'll find many curious rooms in the mansion, like this one with a pair of stairs.

WORLD OF KERALIS, VISIT OR JOIN

SMP, Server

If you love to build, joining a creative building server may be the thing for you. Keralis is a popular Minecraft builder and YouTuber. His public creative Minecraft server, World of Keralis (Keralis.net), is open for Minecraft builders to apply to create buildings for the server's sprawling cities. There are also regular building contests! The builds here can be truly amazing, and you can just join to take a stroll (or fly—this is a creative world) around to see for yourself at Hub.worldofkeralis.com. You can apply to be a builder, or use a guest plot to build on.

You'll find tons of inspiring city and town builds in the World of Keralis server.

WORLD RECORD, CHALLENGE AND BEAT A MINECRAFT

SSP, SMP, Competition

There are world records in the real world, and there are world records in Minecraft too! Different organizations keep track of the challenge attempts to beat a world record. Two organizations tracking Minecraft records are Guinness World Records and RecordSetter.

The Guinness World Records includes the Longest Tunnel Created in Minecraft (100,000 blocks long!) and the Fastest Time to Build a Minecraft House (3:54). There are over 150 total Guinness World Records for Minecraft. To view all of these, you'll need to sign up for an account and use their advanced record search. Some records are still open to be broken, and you can apply to enter your record. There are fees for priority applications and fees for creating a brand-new record title. Go

to Guinnessworldrecords.com and search for Minecraft to get started!

Record Setter is an organization designed specifically for custom world records invented by individuals, and currently has ninety-four tracked Minecraft world records, including the Farthest Distance Ridden on a Pig and the very specific, "Most Blocks of Wet Sponge Dropped In Peonies." Go to Recordsetter.com/Minecraft-world-records to see them. Click on an individual record to see more about the record. If you want to beat it, click the "Challenge It!" button. There you'll find all the rules for beating the challenge and sending in your application.

WORLDEDIT, EDIT YOUR WORLD WITH

SSP, Building, Mod

WorldEdit is an invaluable tool for builders and mapmakers. It's a mod that allows you to place thousands of blocks at a time, including custom spheres and cylinders, and even use a mathematical equation to set blocks. You can copy and paste segments of the world or completed builds, build forests, and use a brush tool to build and carve mountains and ravines. Install it like any other mod with MultiMC or the Twitch launcher. As with any mod, you'll

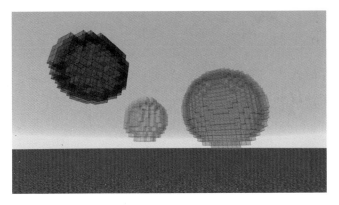

You can create structures and shapes, and smooth or replace blocks in seconds with the World-Edit mod.

need to use the version of Minecraft that the latest version of World-Edit is programmed for, and the version of Forge that works with that Minecraft. There's an excellent wiki that has links to download and explains the World-Edit commands at Wiki.sk89q.wiki/WorldEdit.

WYNNCRAFT, VISIT AND QUEST THROUGH

SMP, Server, Gameplay

Wynncraft is the largest MMORPG (massively multiplayer role-playing game) Minecraft server. It's a public server, free to play, and you'll start out with simple quests and progress through an amazingly detailed custom, hand-built (and very large) map of towns, castles, and kingdoms, with dangers, stories, quests, and adventures for you to explore. Quests and stories will be given to you as you explore. As you gain experience, you can level up to higher ranks. You can even team up with friends to form a guild. Find out more at Wynncraft.com or just open up Multiplayer and use Play.wynncraft.com as the server to join. (Make sure to enable Server Resource Packs.) You'll start off in a lobby area where you can look around and then dive through the giant portal to begin your adventure! There's a lot to take in—from special quest books, choosing a role, spells to learn, enemy levels, and more—so you may want to visit the website to see what's in store. Clicking on NPCs (non-playable characters) can help you find your way also.

Wynncraft is a massive Minecraft world and game on a public server. Your first quest is to find the king, and it's not that easy. Ask characters along the way for advice!

YOUTUBE LET'S PLAYS, WATCH SOME

OOG

A fast way to get inspired is to watch some Minecraft Let's Play videos of popular You-Tubers. Not every Let's Player is for everyone: some may be too loud for you, or not loud enough! But in general, the energy and enthusiasm of Minecraft Let's Players can help give you an idea and the motivation for your next project. If you haven't watched any YouTubers before, take a look at the players on this list. You may find your next favorite Minecraft Let's Play!

Popular, kid-friendly channels include the following (in bold are my personal favorites): Amy Lee33, AntVenom, Aureylian*, **BdoubleO100***, DanTDM, **direwolf20**, **docm77***, **EthosLab**, **FalseSymmetry***, GoodTimesWith-Scar*, iBallisticSquid, iHasCupQuake, Netty Plays, **paulsoaresjr**, PopularMMOs, Preston-Playz, SethBling*, stacyplays, stampylonghead, Thinknoodles, Tiny Turtle & Little Lizard, **VintageBeef***, WelsnightPlays, and xisumavoid.

*In these players' collaborative videos with others, their friends do sometimes swear; they may also play other games with mature themes.

ZOMBIE DOCTOR

Advancement

In this advancement, you must cure a zombie villager. First throw a splash potion of weakness at it, then feed it (right-click it with) a golden apple. The zombie villager will start shaking and the process takes several minutes. You'll want to prevent it from infecting other villagers in the meantime and make sure it is sheltered from the burning sun.

ZOMBIE SIEGE, WITNESS A

SSP, Quest

At midnight, there's a 10 percent chance that a large village (twenty or more villagers and ten or more doors) will experience a zombie siege if you are within the village. There may only be a few or five zombies at a time in the siege, although there could be more. There's nothing you can do to prevent a zombie siege other than staying outside the village at night. During a zombie siege, zombies can spawn at any light level and at any distance from a player and even on transparent blocks like slabs. To witness a zombie siege, you'll want to find a large-enough village and stay in it at midnight.

Zombie sieges will only occur in larger villages.

ZOO, BUILD YOUR OWN

SSP, Quest

Get at least one of every type of mob possible and place them in a zoo. Design the zoo to look like a real zoo, with an entrance, areas for different species, inside shelters for mobs that need it, and rest areas.

Be your own zoo tycoon by building your perfect Minecraft zoo. Will it feature hostile mobs?